The Scotch-Irish

ALSO BY RON CHEPESIUK
AND FROM MCFARLAND

*Hard Target: The United States War Against
International Drug Trafficking, 1982–1997* (1999)

Raising Hell: Straight Talk from Investigative Journalists
(with Haney Howell and Edward Lee; 1997)

*Sixties Radicals, Then and Now: Candid Conversations
with Those Who Shaped the Era* (1995)

The Scotch-Irish

From the North of Ireland to the Making of America

by
RON CHEPESIUK

McFarland & Company, Inc., Publishers
Jefferson, North Carolina, and London

Library of Congress Cataloguing-in-Publication Data

Chepesiuk, Ronald.
    The Scotch-Irish : from the north of Ireland to the making of
America / by Ron Chepesiuk.
      p. cm.
    Includes bibliographical references and index.   ∞
    ISBN 0-7864-0614-3 (illustrated case binding : 50# alkaline paper)
    1. Scots-Irish—United States—History. 2. Scots—Ulster
(Northern Ireland and Ireland)—History. 3. Presbyterians—
United States—History. 4. Presbyterians—Ulster (Northern
Ireland and Ireland)—History. 5. United States—Emigration
and immigration—History. 6. Ulster (Northern Ireland and
Ireland)—Emigration and immigration—History. I. Title.
E184.S4 C47 2000
973'.0491630415—dc21
                                      99-55348

British Library Cataloguing-in-Publication data are available

Manufactured in the United States of America

McFarland & Company, Inc., Publishers
  Box 611, Jefferson, North Carolina 28640
    www.mcfarlandpub.com

For my wife,
Magdalena, with love

Acknowledgments

I express my special thanks to some special people who contributed in numerous ways, but most importantly through their encouragement and enthusiasm for the project.

Dr. Charles B. Vail, former President of Winthrop University, and Shirley M. Tarlton, former Dean of Library Services, gave me permission to spend a sabbatical year in Ireland, which allowed me to do much of the research for the book. Ms. Tarlton was also most supportive during the three years it took to complete the project.

My good friend Dr. Edward Lee, as well as Dr. Fred Hembree, Dr. Ed Clark, Tom Longshaw, Ann Evans, and Jeff Swagger, read the manuscript and offered good criticism and valuable suggestions. Mary L. Brown, Rene Capps, and Kathy Miller patiently deciphered my handwriting and typed earlier drafts of the manuscript. The Winthrop Research Council and the Southern Education Board awarded grants that helped pay for the cost of the project.

The following institutions allowed the author access to their collections and kindly provided assistance in locating information and photographs for the project: The National Library of Ireland, the Ulster Folk Museum, the Northern Ireland Tourist Board, the Winthrop University Archives and Special Collections, and the Reference Department of Winthrop University's Dacus Library.

As head of the Winthrop University Archives, I have come in contact with a host of people of Scotch-Irish ancestry. My thanks go to them for providing the inspiration to write the book.

Table of Contents

Preface

This book is about the Scotch-Irish, or Ulster Scots, as they are commonly known in Ireland. The Scotch-Irish were originally lowland Scots who migrated in considerable numbers to the province of Ulster in Ireland in the seventeenth century to participate in the colonial scheme established during the reign of James I (1603–25) and then in the next century, because of economic and religious reasons, emigrated once more to America by the thousands. Next to the English, the Scotch-Irish were the largest ethnic group to come to the New World during the eighteenth century. By the time of the American Revolution, some historians have estimated, as many as 250,000 Scotch-Irish may have been in the colonies, about one out of ten Americans.

Upon arriving, they began to play their part in the making of America, influencing the country's political, educational, and religious development. They were instrumental in establishing the Presbyterian religion, providing impetus to elementary schools and colleges, and initiating political change. During the American Revolution, the Scotch-Irish swelled the ranks of the Continental Army. Many contemporaries attested to their fighting ability and fervent support of the patriot cause. One Hessian captain, for example, wrote in 1778, "Call this war by whatever name you may, only call it not an American rebellion; it is nothing more or less than a Scotch-Irish Presbyterian rebellion." After the war, the Scotch-Irish formed the vanguard in the westward expansion of the young nation into the trans–Allegheny region and beyond.

1

Preface

They came to America as Presbyterians, but later, after adapting to their new home, the Scotch-Irish joined the Baptist, Lutheran, and other Protestant sects. In a recent study, the National Opinion Research Center in Chicago produced statistics showing that 12 percent of all adult Americans name Ireland as the country from which most of their ancestors came. Surprisingly, 56 percent of these said that they were members of the Protestant Church. Since the overwhelming number of Protestants who emigrated from Ireland to America were Scotch-Irish, this means that out of an estimated 40 million people of Irish background in America, perhaps over 20 million are of Scotch-Irish ancestry.

Despite their numbers and their contributions, the Scotch-Irish story is not well known. A primary reason is that the Scotch-Irish were easily absorbed into mainstream America. They adjusted quickly to their new home and made no conscious effort to maintain a separate identity as other ethnic groups have done. This assimilation is evidenced today by the fact that we can find no strong traditions and customs celebrated by the Scotch-Irish—ancestors of those Scots who came to America via Ireland during the eighteenth and early nineteenth centuries.

Much of what has been written about the Scotch-Irish has tended to glorify their legacy, emphasizing the notable personality at the expense of the anonymous masses who make up most of the people. Although it is interesting to learn that a number of Scotch-Irishmen had a role to play in the drafting of the Declaration of Independence and that several became presidents, this type of history does little to help us understand the Scotch-Irish contribution to the broad sweep of American history.

Some good scholarly works on Scotch-Irish history have appeared. R. S. Dickson's *Ulster Emigration to Colonial America, 1718–1775* (1976), M. Perceval-Maxwell's *The Scottish Migration in Ulster in the Reign of James I* (1973), and James G. Leyburn's *The Scotch-Irish: A Social History* (1962) have all helped to dispel myths and put the Scotch-Irish story in perspective.

This book is not intended to be another laudatory history.

Rather, it is written for the general reader who is interested in learning about the major factors and events that have influenced the history of the Scotch-Irish people.

I begin the Scotch-Irish story at a much earlier date than do most other authors, who usually start with the migration of the lowland Scots to Ireland in the seventeenth century to participate in the colonial scheme of James I. Before the Ulster Plantation, Scotland and Ireland interacted for centuries. The first chapter will help explain later events in Irish and Scottish history that had a bearing on the Scotch-Irish story. Subsequent chapters deal with the life of the Scotch-Irish in Ireland, their treatment by their English overlords, their reasons for emigration to America, the places where the Scotch-Irish settled in America, the movement westward across America, their life on the colonial frontier, the contributions the Scotch-Irish have made to America's development, and sites of Scotch-Irish interest in the north of Ireland.

I hope this book will help the reader gain a better appreciation and understanding of the history and contributions of one of the major groups to shape the early development of the United States.

Prologue

Going to America: The Thomas Mellon Experience

In the second half of the nineteenth century, Thomas Mellon rose to wealth and power as a famous American entrepreneur who built the foundation for what became—and still is—one of the largest family fortunes in the United States. Mellon started out as a lawyer but quickly realized that his adopted country offered more lucrative prospects for a financier, and so he invested money, bought property, and even opened his own bank. When he died in 1908, Mellon's fortune was put at $4 million.[1]

Throughout his life, as he climbed the American ladder of success, Thomas never forgot how it had all begun, and he took pride in the fact that his parents and family had come from Ulster in the north of Ireland and that his roots were Scotch-Irish.

Mellon's life began like that of many other thousands of Scotch-Irish who migrated to the United States in the eighteenth and nineteenth centuries—in a humble, whitewashed, one-room cottage on a small farm in rural northern Ireland. Thomas's father, Andrew, and his uncle Archie had built the cottage at the foot of Camphill, Lower Castletown, Parish of Cappaigh, County Tyrone, a few years before Thomas was born on February 3, 1813.

Although Thomas was only five years old when he and his

family set sail from Londonderry to the United States, the memory of those formative years remained vivid, with all of "its details of location and scenery."[2]

In 1816, Thomas's grandfather had emigrated to Greensburg in Westmoreland County, Pennsylvania, joining his uncle who had settled in Philadelphia.[3] Thomas and his parents waited for the letters from their relatives in America with great anticipation and excitement, and they held long family gatherings at night, discussing and debating the pros and cons of emigrating to the New World.

"I ... remember the long winter nights which were spent by my parents perusing and discussing descriptions of different parts of America, and the products of the land, and the opportunities for bettering the conditions of settlers there," Thomas Mellon wrote in his autobiography.[4]

It took two years for the Mellon family to make the decision to leave Ulster, and then, as Thomas later recalled, "came much talk and consultation about selling the farm and disposing of the stock and the settling of affairs. It all resulted in the aggregation of about two hundred guineas in gold coin, equal to one thousand dollars. They were carefully stored in a belt which my mother fastened around her waist, with which to sink or swim as the case might be in our voyage over the stormy sea."[5]

And so the day of departure finally arrived, and the family set sail from Londonderry, making an arduous twelve-week voyage to St. Johns, New Brunswick. "All I remember of St. Johns is seeing fields covered with fish split open to dry," Mellon later wrote. "And here I saw and tasted the cucumber and saw negroes."[6]

The Mellon family obtained passage in another ship and set sail for Baltimore, Maryland, landing at the city in October 1818. After a few uneventful days, the Mellons chartered a Conestoga wagon and a team of four horses and set out for Greensburg in search of their relatives. The tiring journey through the mountains took three weeks, but upon arrival the weary emigrants had a joyful family reunion with grandparents, uncles, and aunts.

The Mellons bought a modest farm and began the difficult

task of making a new life for themselves. It was not easy; indeed, in 1819 an economic depression nearly wiped our their finances. The life, though, was one that had a happy home as its foundation, and the love and security encouraged Thomas to adopt the attitude and determined spirit that would eventually make him one of nineteenth-century America's most successful businessmen.

"No home can be unhappy to a boy with kind parents and good health," Mellon later recalled. "His work may be severe with few indulgences and little time to play or recreation; but ... good health and kindness at home, the exuberance of boyish spirits, and the anticipation of a better time coming will supply the necessary pleasure and enjoyment."[7]

After some struggle and sacrifice, the better time did come, and in the words of young Thomas, his family "was put in the way of material progress."[8] After graduating with honors from the Western University of Pennsylvania in 1837, Thomas was admitted to the bar. He opened his law office in June 1839 and gradually built up a thriving practice, while shrewdly investing his savings in real estate, coalfields, mortgage and loans, a railway line, and an iron foundry.

In 1843, he married Pittsburg socialite Sarah Jane Negley after a long courtship, and they had eight children during the next seventeen years. The bank he founded in 1870 with his sons Thomas Alexander and James Ross became the foundation for one of the nation's most powerful financial institutions. Eventually, Thomas Mellon garnered distinction as one of Pittsburgh's most prominent and honored citizens. As the *National Cyclopedia of American Biography* noted, "It was said of Mellon that never in his entire life did he fail in any undertaking to which he seriously devoted himself."[9]

Yet throughout the successes and up until his death in 1908, Thomas Mellon remained nostalgic for his childhood home in the north of Ireland. He even built a replica of the Camphill cottage in the backyard of his family home in Pittsburg, and at night he would sit with his wife at the fireside in the replica cottage and reminisce.

In 1882, Thomas Mellon finally visited his boyhood home and was delighted to learn that it was much like he remembered it. "There was not the slightest correction to be made to my mental map," Mellon recalled. "It was all there in every particular as I had seen it when I was a child and still recalled it."[10]

During the first half of the twentieth century, however, the cottage fell on hard times, and by the 1950s, it had become a farm building for pigs and for storing hay. The Mellon family retained a strong interest in the site, and with their support, the house was restored and opened to the public in 1968 as part of the Ulster American Folk Park.

The dedication's opening ceremonies were the occasion of a Mellon family reunion, with some fifty members of one of America's richest families gathering at Camphill. The government and people of Northern Ireland treated the family like visiting royalty. The Northern Ireland government provided Cadillacs for those Mellons who needed transportation and even found a partner for one of the Mellons who wanted to play a game of tennis.

Thomas Mellon, the gathering knew, was just one of Northern Ireland's many famous native sons who had joined the great emigrant waves of the eighteenth and nineteenth centuries. Among those emigrants were the ancestors of Andrew Jackson, Chester Alan Arthur, William McKinley, and several other U.S. presidents; John Dunlap, the founder of America's first newspaper; Horace Greeley, the founder of the *New York Herald Tribune*; and David Crockett, the great frontiersman.[11]

The dedication ceremony came 150 years after Thomas Mellon and his family set sail for the New World. Northern Ireland Prime Minister Terence O'Neill noted the significance of the occasion: "This home will forever be a monument not just to the Mellon family but to the potential of human character in the land of opportunity."[12]

1

Ireland and Scotland Before the Plantation

The story of the Mellons and the many other Scotch-Irish who came to America from the north of Ireland and the province known as Ulster in search of a better life really begins long before Scottish settlers began emigrating to Ireland in the early seventeenth century to participate in the colonial scheme of James I. Ireland and Scotland are political entities shaped in the modern era. For centuries the area encompassing Ireland and Scotland was a vast cultural sea, which experienced a continuous intermingling of its people and a sharing of traditions. In light of the fact that at the narrowest part of the North Channel, Scotland is a mere twelve miles from the Irish coast and is plainly visible on a clear day, it is not surprising that there has been close contact since earliest times.

The evidence of archaeology, anthropology, and mythology and the occasional reference in fragments of early written records help to document the Scotch-Irish relationship. It is now commonly believed that Ireland's first inhabitants, the people of the Mesolithic period, arrived over nine thousand years ago via the Scottish route.

When the Romans occupied the British Isles during the early Christian period, the historian Tacitus revealed that his father-in-law, Agricola, while encamped with Roman legions on the Scottish coast across from the Irish counties of Antrim and Down, gave refuge to a petty Irish king who had been chased from his own country because of a domestic quarrel.[1] Modern place-name studies indicate that settlers from the north of Ireland made their homes in the west of Scotland long before the dominance of the region from the eighth to the tenth centuries by the Vikings. And the early Irish annals contain entries that many archaeologists believe are Scottish.[2]

Those who came from the north of Ireland to colonize western Scotland, beginning in the fifth century, brought their traditions of the region with them, and these ancient traditions endured in Scotland long after their disappearance from the greater part of Ireland. Well into the twentieth century, folk material originating in the north of Ireland could still be collected in the highlands and islands of Scotland. The interaction of the Scots and Irish through the centuries produced a common heritage of poetry and music. Irish pipers and harpists, for example, carried to Scotland airs that are today regarded as traditional Scottish tunes. In the famous collection of poems known as *The Book of the Dun of Lismore*, twenty-one out of sixty-five poems were authored by Irishmen.[3]

The northern part of Ireland in which the Scots settled and from where they later migrated to America has traditionally been called Ulster. Along with Leinster, Munster, and Connacht, it is one of the four provinces of Ireland. Historically, there was a fifth province, Meath, but this territory had consolidated with the other four by the seventeenth century. Today, "Ulster" is used by many Irish Protestants as a name substitute for Northern Ireland, although the British colony includes only six of the original nine Ulster counties. Historic Ulster comprised these six (Fermanagh, Armagh, Antrim, Down, Tyrone, and Londonderry), as well as Monaghan, Donegal, and Cavan, now part of the Republic of Ireland.

Before Scottish settlers brought a new culture and religion to Ulster, geography gave the province a distinctive character and tradition, helping it to stand apart from the rest of Ireland. For much of history, vast tracts of woodlands, as well as rivers, lakes, bogs, and drumlins (small hills), provided Ulster with a natural border and a strong defensive barrier against incursions from the south. As a result, the province developed separately, with its own unique identity.[4] In fact, geographically, Ulster has much more in common with Scotland. Its mountains are like Scotland's, their ridges running in a northeast and southwest direction. Those of southern Ireland, on the other hand, run in an east-west direction and are similar to the ranges of Spain, Wales, and France.

Ulster derives its name from the ancient tribe of Ulaid, which had its center at Navan, near Armagh, and inhabited the northeast part of Ireland in the early Christian period. At the height of its power, this northern kingdom extended as far south as the Boyne River. The Ulaid were a rural people who had a decentralized political and social structure based on the family and local lordships and who were constantly at war with the rulers of other provinces, as the various Irish kings fought to be "ard ri," or high king, of Ireland. Under the aggressive leadership of Niall of the Nine Hostages, the greatest of the Connacht kings, who served as the ard ri from A.D. 380 to 405, the western part of Ulster was conquered and colonized by his sons Conall and Eogan.[5] In the process, the Ulaid were driven east of the Bann, where they established a new life as rulers of the modern counties of Antrim and Down.

Across the narrow strip of sea, in the early Christian period, stood the Romans. Although they had conquered the British Isles by the third century A.D., the Romans never tried to make the short journey to Ireland and add the Emerald Isle to their empire; in fact, there is no evidence that one Roman soldier ever set foot on the island. To the Romans, Ireland was known as "Scotia" and its inhabitants, "Scotti," or as we would say today, "Scots." This name stayed with the Celtic tribes of Ireland despite the fact that they referred to themselves in their own language as "Gaels." As the Roman Empire disintegrated under the pressure of the barbarian hordes, the Romans gradually withdrew their forces from the British Isles.

It was during this period of transition that the Scots first began to make their presence felt outside Ireland: as fierce marauding warriors plundering England, Wales, and the western coast of Scotland. So notorious did the Scots become that their name became synonymous with "raider."[6] Many other Scots, including the mighty Niall of the Nine Hostages, came to help their fellow Scots against their arch enemies, the Picts.

By the third century A.D., the Scots began to cross the North Channel, not as raiders or fighters but as colonists. It began with Cabri Riada, one of the three sons of the high king Conaire the Great. The Irish annals tell us that Cabri led a large number of people from Munster in southwest Ireland, where famine was rampant, to County Antrim in the northeast. After conquering the local inhabitants, Cabri established the kingdom of Dalriada. But Cabri was an ambitious man, and soon after, in A.D. 258, he crossed the sea and established Scottish Dalriada in modern day Argyll. The rock fort of Dunadd, situated in middle Argyll and a strategic fortress since Iron Age times, became the capital of the new colony.

As time passed, more and more Scots crossed the Irish Sea to live in the new colony, many of them to help their fellow Scots in their constant battles with their neighbors. In about A.D. 500, for reasons lost in history, a large migration under the leadership of Fergus Mor, son of Erc, took place from Irish Dalriada. Fergus abandoned his base at Dunservik, the capital of Irish Dalriada, for permanent residence in Scotland. Accompanying Fergus were his two brothers, Loarn and Angus. The three brothers divided the Dalriada kingdom between them and established the first district clans in Scotland: Cinel Garran, Cinel Camgall, Cinel Angus, and Cinel Loarn.

Loarn moved into the area that today bears his name. Fergus occupied Kintyre, Knapdale, Cowall, and Mid-Argyll, while Angus controlled Islay. Fergus, as leader of the migration, became the unofficial king of Scottish Dalriada. When Fergus's son Domingart succeeded him in 501, he took the title Ri Alban, or King of Alba (Scotland).

During the early years following this significant movement of people, there was constant communication between Scottish Dalriada and the parent colony. Eventually, however, the offspring grew stronger than the parent and began to enjoy certain privileges with regard to military service and taxation. The gradual dominance of Scottish Dalriada resulted in disagreements that necessitated a conference in 575 at Drumceatt near the town of Limavady in County Londonderry. Scottish Dalriada made important concessions, leading to a peaceful severance of ties between the two Dalriadas. Irish Dalriada gradually declined in influence and power, and with the defeat of its ruler Domnall Breac by the kings of Ireland at the Battle of Mora in 637, it no longer constituted a force to be reckoned with.

Just the opposite occurred in western Scotland. Scottish Dalriada not only consolidated its holdings but rapidly grew in power and territory. One historian has said, "A constant factor in the history of the Scots from the period of migration from Ireland right through the 12th century was their urge to expand into new territories."[7] This they did at the expense of their neighbors. Post-Roman Scotland included not only the Scots but also three other groups: Picts, Britains, and Angles. Among the four, there was constant warfare and a continuous changing of borders or, as one writer has put it, "murder, marriage, truce, treachery."[8] From their stronghold in Argyll, the Scots eventually controlled the islands of Arran, Islay, Jura, Colmsay, Iona, and part of the Mull of Tiree. By the beginning of the fifth century, they had pushed eastward, occupying the district known as Fifshire.

The migration of the Scots from Ireland was the most significant event in Scotland's early history. By the twelfth century, Scotland and its people had taken the name of the immigrant. Gaelic, the language of the Scots of Ireland, eventually became the language of much of Scotland. Even today it is still spoken in western Scotland. The colonists also gave Scotland their kings. From Fergus Mor, with a few early exceptions, descended all the kings and queens of Scotland down to the present day.

According to tradition, Fergus brought with him a stone used by Jacob as a pillow at Bethel. Called the Lia Fail or Stone of Destiny, it had been kept at the Cashel Cathedral in Ireland, where it was used by the kings of Ireland as their coronation seat. Beginning with Kenneth I. MacAlpin, this tradition was carried on by the kings of Scotland. He moved the stone to the Pictish center of Scone for his 843 coronation. In 1296 it was taken by King Edward I to England, where it has been kept at Westminster Abbey ever since. Perhaps more important were the Irish monks who wandered far from their homeland and played a prominent role in converting Scotland and other western European countries to Christianity. The first organized Christian church in Scotland or Ireland was founded by one of these monks, Saint Ninian, in A.D. 397 at Whithorn in the southern Galloway region of Scotland. He named his church Candida Casa (White House), and to this day, traces of the church are still in evidence. To this retreat came a constant procession of Irish monks, who received training and education and then returned to their native land to share what they had learned with their brethren.

In the fifth century, it was Saint Patrick who began the task of converting Ireland to Christianity. The details of the life of Ireland's Patron Saint are cloaked in legend. Many believe he was born in Britain or in Gaul, while others claim that his birthplace was near the Firth of the Clyde in Scotland. Kidnapped by slave traders at age fourteen, Patrick was carried off to Ireland, where he spent six years as a herdsman, either in County Antrim or County Mayo. After escaping and making his way to Gaul, Patrick studied for the priesthood and then returned to Ireland in 431. The next year he became bishop of Ireland and began the task of establishing churches and religious communities. His cathedral church of Armagh in Ulster became the spiritual and administrative center of the Irish church.

Saint Patrick's pioneering work served as an inspiration to others. An Irish monk named Finbar studied at Candida Casa for twenty years and then returned to establish a monastery in County Down. Another monastery, founded by Saint Columgall in 538 at Bangor in the Ards, became one of the foremost missionary centers of the Irish church, and from it came a steady stream of zealous workers to the shores of Scotland.

By the end of the sixth century, however, the Christian church was in shambles as Europe entered the Dark Ages. Ireland now became an outpost of Christianity as, during the next several centuries, the Irish monks played a major part in preserving learning and the cultural tradition of the West by writing books and developing libraries and centers of learning. Although many of the books were written in Latin, the official language of the church, the traditional literature and numerous religious treatises were written in Irish.

The production of books was considered such an important task that a special place inside the monastery, called the *scriptoria*, was used. The traditional literature of the period refers to monastic libraries. *The Martyrology of Oengus Felire (Engus)*, written in about 800, mentions a library of Saint Longarad of Ossory in the sixth century, describing it as a collection of books of all the sciences. Later, in the tenth century, the *Annals of Tigennach* refers to a large library in Clonmacnoise.

During the seventh and eighth centuries, the monks refined the art of illuminating the magnificent books they produced. The art reached its most magnificent expression in the *Book of Kells*, considered by many to be the world's most beautiful book. It is believed that this cultural treasure was actually started on the island of Iona but was then taken to the Irish monastery of Kells during the Viking invasions of the late 700s. The story of the *Book of Kells* is found in the *Annals of Ulster* (1007), which says, "On account of its secular cover it was stolen by night from the great stone church of Cenannus."[9] The *Book of Kells* is now safely preserved in the famous Long Room of Trinity College, Dublin. Other fine examples of the art of illumination now crowd the shelves of such libraries in Ireland as the National Library and the Royal Irish Academy Library. When the Irish monks traveled to Britain and the continent to preach the gospel, they carried books with them, and many can now be found in the archives and libraries of many European countries.

The Irish monks were eager to leave their native country and travel abroad, spreading the faith as "pilgrims of Christ": this was considered the highest penance. Two of the more prominent of these monks were Saint Canice, the patron saint of the Irish town of Kilkenny, who worked in Scotland as a missionary for several years and eventually built a church at a place that became known as St. Andrews, and Saint Kierman who worked hard in the service of the church on the peninsula of Kintyre during the sixth century.

The most celebrated Irish monk to cross the sea to Scotland was Saint Columba. He could have had the easy life, if he had so chosen. Columba was born of royal blood in Donegal, the scion of the O'Neill family, the most powerful in Ireland at the time. After establishing two important monasteries at Durrow and Derry, Columba, he decided, for reasons not entirely clear, to leave Ireland for Scotland. Tradition says that in 561 a quarrel flared over a manuscript he had copied. In a time when manuscripts were rare and valuable, this was regarded as a serious offense. The matter was brought before High King Diarmart, whose ruling satisfied no one and precipitated war between the king and Columba's own clan. Disgusted with the bloodshed he had caused, Columba left Ireland in 563, never to return.

Columba's journey eventually took him to Iona, a small primitive island on Mull's west coast. He was forty-two years old; his next thirty-six years were spent developing Iona into a center of missionary activity and the heart of an expanding ecclesiastical empire. From this base, Columba sent his followers to convert the pagans of Scotland, England, France, Switzerland, Germany, and Italy. Since Iona stood in the heart of Dalriada, Columba was quick to establish close relationships with the territory's rulers. Aidan, the great-grandson of Fergus Mor and king of Dalriada from 574 to 608, received counsel and support from Columba and was consecrated king of Dalriada at Iona in 574, the earliest documentary reference to a ceremony of ordination of a king on the British Isles. The next year Columba accompanied Aidan to a conference at Drumceatt, where the political autonomy of Irish Dalriada was discussed. After a year's negotiation, it was ruled that Aed, the high king of Ireland, would have the allegiance of the Irish Dalriada, while King Aidan would have hegemony over Scottish Dalriada. Later, Columba advised Aidan about which of his sons should succeed him as king.

Scottish Dalriada continued to grow, winning many of the battles fought with the Picts, absorbing the latter's land and slowly smothering their culture and customs. Over a period of time, the Scots and Picts became fused, with many of the Pictish kings sitting on the Dalriadic throne and some of the Scottish kings bearing Pictish names. This fusion began in 843 when Kenneth, son of Alpin, king of the Scots, with the help of military reinforcements from Ireland, decisively defeated the Picts. In order to take firmer control of his vastly expanded territories, the conquering Kenneth transferred the seat of royal government from Dalriada to Scone, the sacred capital of Pictland. So dominant became the influence of the Scots that the Picts all but disappeared from history. Today, we know little about them or about Pictish laws, traditions, and language. Only a few place names give evidence to their existence.

Communication between Ireland and Scotland was disrupted by Viking invasions that began in the eighth century and continued for the next three hundred years. The name "Viking" is an Old Norse word meaning sea-rover or pirate and was a generic term applied to the Swedes, Danes, and Norwegians who launched raids along the coast of the British Isles and Ireland and as far east as Moscow and Constantinople. These fearless seamen devised adaptable boats that gave them a military advantage over their enemies. The boats not only could travel long distances in the deep, rough waters of the North Atlantic but easily navigated the shallow waters of inland river systems as well.

After quickly conquering Greenland and Iceland, the Vikings moved on to the Hebrides and Orkney Islands off the north coast of Scotland; by 794, they had reached and plundered Iona. Periodic raids forced the monks to flee to Ireland and the monastery at Kells. So unsafe were the times that the remains of Saint Columba were removed from Iona. Seven years later a group of monks were massacred for their refusal to reveal Saint Columba's burial site.

The Vikings continued their onslaught, pillaging the small monastery communities off the islands of Ireland and establishing colonies, which they used as bases to attack the Irish mainland. The rugged Ulster coastline, however, discouraged the Vikings from conquest of the north. With the exception of a few place-names such as Olderfleet, Strangford, and Carlingford, the Vikings left little of permanence. But in southern Ireland, Viking settlements became Ireland's first cities: Dublin in 841, followed by Cork, Limerick, Wexford, Waterford, and Wicklow. From these strongholds, the Vikings pushed deep into the interior of Ireland, plundering the great monasteries and stealing gold and other valuables. Weak and divided, the Irish could do little to stop the advances of their indomitable foes.

The Viking dominance of Ireland continued until Brian Boru became high king in 1002. Under Brian's leadership, Irish resistance stiffened. All through his life, he showed a stubborn determination not to back down from the invaders. By the age of forty, Brian had become king of Cashel, thus giving himself complete control of southern Ireland. A series of stunning victories elevated Brian to the office of high king, although his family lineage did not entitle him to this position. He worked hard to unite Ireland politically and to restore the country to its former position of religious learning, rebuilding the churches and monasteries and even sending scholars to the continent to find books for the plundered libraries.

Alarmed at Brian's increasing power, a secret alliance was forged between disgruntled Viking vassals in Dublin and Brian's archenemy, the king of Lienster. They sought help from Sigurd the Stout (the earl of Orkney), who agreed to supply two thousand troops in return for the promise of the high kingship of Ireland, if the alliance was victorious. The decisive battle was fought on Good Friday, April 23, 1014, just outside Dublin's walls. Brian, now in his seventies, was too old to fight, so he watched from an encampment while his son, Murchadh, commanded his forces. At dawn the fighting began; by nightfall, the Vikings had been driven back to Clontarf and the sea, where an exceptionally high tide was drowning them by the hundreds before they could reach the safety of their ships. During the retreat, one Viking captain named Brodir fled into the woods. He came upon the great high king Brian in his tent. With one accurate swing of the ax, the Viking split the old warrior's head open. Later captured, Brodir paid for his deed in the most horrible manner. The story of *Brunt Njal*, the Icelandic saga that provides the most interesting account of the battle, states: "Brodir was taken alive. Ulf Hreda slit open his belly and unwound his intestines from his stomach by leading him round and round an oak tree; and Brodir did not die until they had all been pulled out of him."[10]

The Battle of Clontarf put an end to the Vikings' power and their dream of making Ireland a satellite province. Too weak militarily to continue raiding the interior, they mainly confined themselves to the towns that they had founded. Gradually, the Vikings became absorbed into the Irish way of life, taking Irish wives and adapting the customs, dress, religion, and language of the natives.

The next great invaders of Ireland were the Normans, who came in the late twelfth century. The Normans, who were Vikings too, had established themselves early in the tenth century in a large area around the lower Seine River in France. They were formally granted the territory as the Duchy of the Northmen, which later became know as Normandy. During the next 150 years they acquired a warrior reputation as they added to their holdings, especially in southern Italy. In 1066 William, duke of Normandy, with a small force of five thousand men, conquered England. By 1160, when Dermot MacMurrough, the Irish king of Leinster, was having trouble with his archenemy Tiernan O'Ruark, Prince of Breifne, the Normans were firmly rooted in the British Isles.

MacMurrough's problems began when he ran off with O'Ruark's wife and made the big mistake of going against custom by not paying the high king compensation for her. Because of MacMurrough's indiscretion, O'Ruark was able to obtain the support of many Irish chiefs in Leinster and defeat MacMurrough in battle. MacMurrough heard of the military power of the Normans, and so he traveled to France to the court of Henry II at Aquitaine, where he swore fealty to the Norman king. In return, Henry granted MacMurrough permission to seek support of the Norman barons to help him recover his throne. In southwest Wales he found a willing ally in Richard de Clare, second earl of Pembroke, known as Richard Strongbow, who agreed to help in return for the promise of MacMurrough's daughter in marriage and the succession to the kingship of Leinster.

On May 1, 1169, three ships containing 300 archers, 30 knights, and 60 other horsemen landed at Barrow Bay in County Wexford. After capturing the town of Wexford, the invaders established a strong base at Baginbun. In August 1170 Strongbow landed at Crook near Waterford with 200 knights and 1,000 soldiers. A few days later, after capturing Waterford, Strongbow was joined by MacMurrough and his daughter, whom Strongbow quickly married. Within a month, Strongbow was in complete control of Leinster.

When MacMurrough died in May 1171, Strongbow claimed his throne, but the Leinster Irish refused to accept him, since his claim was contrary to Brehon law, which provided for the king's election. Strongbow's enemies in Leinster joined forces with Rory O'Connor, whose army, now greatly strengthened, was soon able to besiege Dublin. So effective was the Irish pressure that Strongbow offered to surrender and "to become his man and hold Leinster of him."[11] O'Connor refused. However, the Normans were able to withstand the siege, take the offensive, and rout O'Connor's army.

Meanwhile, Henry was watching Ireland's state of affairs with some concern, lest Strongbow and the other Norman barons who accompanied him had thoughts about establishing independent principalities of their own. To protect his interest, Henry now decided to come to Ireland. In October 1171, Henry landed with a fleet of 400 ships and about 4,000 troops. Henry's powerful force impressed many of the Irish chiefs, and they quickly submitted to him. Henry summoned a synod of Cashel, where the Irish church gave its support and pledged to conform to the practices of the English church. The Norman king also received the backing of the pope, who instructed the Irish bishops to support Henry's rule in Ireland and conferred upon him the title of "Lord of Ireland." In 1175 the proud Irish chieftain Rory O'Connor traveled to England to swear allegiance.

With the situation seemingly under firm control, Henry returned to England, leaving his deputy, Hugh de Lacy, in charge. But with Henry's presence no longer a deterring factor, the barons moved quickly to reap the fruits of victory. Lacy lost no time in awarding himself a large chunk of County Meath; the rest of the county was divided up by his officers. Another baron, John de Courci, set out from Dublin with a small force and carved out a princely domain in northeast Ulster. Although failing to penetrate beyond the Bann River, Courci did manage to build towns, castles, and monasteries at Downpatrick, Newry, Coleraine, and the Carrickfergus. When King John landed with his army in 1185, he set about granting to his followers land that was supposedly guaranteed to the Irish kings. From these grants emerged some of the great Anglo-Irish families: the Butlers, the Burkes, and the Fitzgeralds, to name a few of the most prominent.

The Irish were no match for the Normans and could do little to stop their conquest. Military superiority and sophistication were the reasons. While the Irish soldier went into battle wearing only a linen tunic, his Norman counterpart clad himself in armor from head to foot. The Norman warrior fought from horseback using long lances, while skilled archers provided support by cutting down the enemy from a distance with the longbow and crossbow. Against the well-armed enemy, the Irish soldier went into battle with only a sword, a spear, or a long ax. The Normans, unlike the Irish, used battle strategy. Just as they did in England and Wales, the Normans consolidated each gain with a castle, made first of earth and timber and later of stone. In contrast, the Irish had no plans. Once the enemy was defeated, they simply devastated the land and left the area.

So, after eighty years of continuous fighting, over two-thirds of Ireland was in Norman possession. The Irish offered no organized resistance against the Norman advance. They quarreled and fought among themselves and even on occasion called on the Normans to help them battle their fellow countymen. However, by the second half of the thirteenth century, the Irish were slowly beginning to realize that cooperation was the only chance they had to defeat the enemy. In 1258 many Irish chiefs backed Brian O'Neill, the senior member of the great Ulster family, as king of all Ireland. Soon after, however, the Irish were at it again, quarreling among themselves as the united front broke down.

Unsuccessful on their own, the Irish began to seek military assistance outside of the island. They looked to the highlands of Scotland and began recruiting professional fighting men known as "gallow glasses." Of mixed Viking and Gaelic descent, these organized bands of mercenary soldiers first hired out their services in the north, but gradually they moved throughout the island and played a significant part in Irish battles for several generations. They were much better armed than their Irish comrades and were more of a match for the Normans. They wore helmets and long chain armor, which was carried by servants when they were not in battle. Their principal weapon was a heavy battle-ax that had a six-foot handle.

Soon after the gallow glasses' arrival, the English began to worry about the presence of these skilled, professional soldiers who at any time could be used against them by rebellious Irish chieftains. Beginning in 1310, a series of acts were passed that were "directed against the keeping of undue numbers of hired men by these lords to whom the English law applied or was supposed to apply."[12] But the gallow glass had become such an accepted part of Irish military practice that to try to abolish the mercenary scheme proved impossible. The Scottish mercenary soldier remained a concern of the English up until the sixteenth century. As late as 1562, the earl of Essex, in a report to the monarch, recommended that "a book be kept by the military for every county in which might be entered the names of all the mercenaries within the area, such book to be delivered to the government each year."[3] But the English could only compromise. At times, they even adopted the Irish practice of hiring out the services of the gallow glasses.

In the second half of the sixteenth century, the gallow glass was succeeded by another type of Scottish soldier known as the Redshank. Unlike the gallow glasses, the Redshanks confined their activities to the north, hired themselves out to the highest bidder, remained for shorter periods of time, and returned to Scotland once their military service was complete. The Redshanks became especially active during the Irish resistance to the Tudor conquest, but after the English victory in 1603, their services came to an end.

By the fourteenth century, Norman expansion had reached its limits. Many of the Irish chiefs took advantage of a weakening English position to regain their lands. In 1333 William, the young earl of Ulster, was murdered by his own tenants, and the entire north once again came under control of the O'Neills. In the south, the two cousins of the murdered earl, Edmond and Ulick de Burgh, seized control and divided the province between them. They changed their name to McWilliam Burke and adopted the Irish customs, language, dress, and laws, paying little heed to the dictates of the Dublin government. In Leinster too, the Anglo-Irish received a setback when Donal Kavanagh proclaimed himself king.

One of the main reasons for the weak Norman position was that not enough settlers had come from England to strengthen the Norman presence. Even in areas of the country where Norman control was strongest, the bulk of the population was Irish. As time passed, the Normans began to become much like the natives, adopting their language, habit, and dress.

So concerned did the authorities become about the worsening state of affairs in Ireland that in 1366 they introduced the Statutes of Kilkenny, which legislated against the use of Irish law and language and the wearing of Irish hairstyles and clothes and tried to keep the Irish and Normans apart. Intermarriage was now a capital offense. The Irish were put in the position of second-class citizens. If they lived within an English colony, they had to speak English. They could not enter their own abbeys and cathedrals. The statutes even went so far as to prevent the Anglo-Irish from playing Irish games or selling the native Irish horses or armor. Although the statutes remained on the books for more than two centuries, they did little to prevent the continual assimilation of the Anglo-Irish. The Normans (now referred to as the Anglo-Irish) continued to fraternize and intermarry with the Irish.

Rebellions became more frequent. From the mid-fourteenth century onward, only Dublin and a small area around it—an area subsequently known as Pale—remained faithful to the Crown. The Pale continued to shrink until, by the 1550s, it was described as "cramped and crouched into an old corner of the country named Fingal, with a part of the king's land of Meath and the counties, of Kildare and Louth."[14]

The gradual weakening of the English position in Ireland can be seen in the fourteenth century when the first substantial and effective Scottish plantation in northern Ireland took place. Unlike the Scots who came later, in the seventeenth century, to participate in the James I plantation scheme, these settlers came from the highlands, not the lowlands, and were Catholic, not Protestant, in religion. In the twelfth century, a number of Norman families had settled in the coastal areas of Counties Antrim and Down. In about 1300, one of these families purchased a large tract of land, two-thirds of what is today the Glens of Antrim. In 1399 Margery Byset, the heiress to the property, married John Mor MacDonnell of Isla, Scotland. The son of this marriage became the lord of Antrim and lord of the Isles, and thus County Antrim from Larne northward passed into the hands of the MacDonnells. During the next two centuries, these Scottish highlanders established several settlements in this part of Ulster. Eventually, the English came to regard these Scots as a threat to the authority of the English Crown. Consequently, legislation was passed during Queen Mary's reign forbidding the "bringing in of Scots, retaining them and marrying with them." Another act made it a felony for anyone in Ireland to marry a Scot who was not a citizen of Ulster."[15]

The combined MacDonnell lordship lasted through the fifteenth century, when it suffered a crushing defeat at the hands of Scottish King James IV. Much of the Scottish territory of the MacDonnells was gobbled up by the Campbells, MacLeods, and MacLeans. Left with only Islay and some of the smaller islands, many of the MacDonnells crossed the sea, taking refuge in County Antrim and making it their political center.

In Ireland the family remained a formidable military force. In 1550 James MacDonnell, still calling himself the lord of the Isles and supported by a large number of Redshanks from the Hebrides, was battling with the O'Neills of Claneboye and pushing them off their lands. The English considered expelling the MacDonnells from Ireland in 1568 when rumors circulated that the earl of Argyll was planning to invade County Antrim. But the last thing the English wanted was to be drawn into a protracted Scottish clan feud, and so nothing was done. The MacDonnells were finally accepted when Sorley Boy MacDonnell received a grant of land in north Antrim in 1586 from Queen Elizabeth. A few years later, in the early 1600s, Randal MacDonnell, later earl of Antrim, the chief of the clan, settled large numbers of lowland Scots on a tract of land given to him by the English.

It was Robert Bruce's invasion from Scotland that showed the weak foundations of the Norman conquest of Ireland. Despite England's persistent efforts, Scotland had managed to maintain its independence. In 1314 Robert Bruce, king of Scotland, decisively defeated the forces of English King Edward II at the Battle of Bannockburn. During the Scottish fight for independence, Ireland had become one of the main sources of supply for the English army in Scotland. On more than one occasion, the English army had been rescued from certain defeat by the arrival of fresh Irish troops. To stop this source of supply, Bruce decided to open up a second front in Ireland and thus help divert English attention away from Scotland.

In May 1315, Edward Bruce, King Robert's brother, landed with six thousand troops on the Antrim Coast. Many of the Irish chiefs in the north were sympathetic toward the Bruces and their struggle with the English. There is even evidence that before 1315, plans were being made for the invasion. Within twelve months of landing, the Scots were in control of much of Ireland northeast of Dublin and were supported by nearly every powerful Irish family. Many were enthralled by the idea of a United Celtic Kingdom embracing Scotland and Ireland. On May 3, 1316, such an idea looked like a reality when Robert Bruce was crowned king of Ireland at Faughart near Dundalk.

Although a general uprising did occur in Leinster and Munster, Edward remained in Ulster, doing nothing. This inactivity did little for Edward's efforts to maintain the support and allegiance of the Irish. Toward the end of 1317, Edward was joined by his brother Robert and a large army. The two headed south toward Dublin looting, killing, and ravaging the countryside. This "scorched earth" policy further eroded the Bruces' Irish support. The devastation was widespread, and the Irish annals tell us that in "Bruce's time, for three years and a half, falsehood, and famine and homicide filled the country, and undoubtedly men ate each other in Ireland."[16]

When the Scots reached Dublin, the city's defenses discouraged the Bruces from attacking. Instead, they marched southeast, continuing their path of destruction until arriving at Carrickfergus in Ulster. Robert Bruce returned to Scotland, leaving Edward to defend his interests. With his army weakened by the ill-fated southern campaign and famine now widespread throughout Ireland, Edward would do little but remain inactive.

Meanwhile, the English had strengthened their position in Ireland by sending reinforcements under the command of Roger Mortimer. Instead of confronting the Scots in battle, Mortimer shrewdly concentrated his attentions on strengthening his position in the south and making peace with the Irish chiefs. By 1318 Edward had become restless and started another southern march. At Faughart, not far from the scene of his brother's coronation two years before,

Edward was defeated and killed. His head was sent as a present to King Edward II. The Irish—the people whom the Scots were to liberate—rejoiced at Edward Bruce's death. Because of his actions, much of the country was comparable to an underpopulated desert. Many towns had been burned to the ground, starvation was widespread, and the financial resources of the country were drained. Most important, the invasion contributed to the gradual breakdown of the central authority in Ireland. In the local areas, the English could no longer govern with the degree of authority they had enjoyed in the thirteenth century.

Not until the reign of the Tudors, beginning with Henry VIII (1491–1547), did England turn its attentions to Ireland and make a concerted effort to bring the Gaelic chieftains in line as vassals of the crown. Ireland was now under the control of the great Anglo-Irish families—the Fitzgeralds of Kildare, the O'Neills and O'Donnells of Ulster, the Butlers of Ormond, the Fitzgeralds of Desmond, and the MacMurroughs of Leinser—who ran their affairs without much interference from the English authorities. Life outside the Pale was dominated by Gaelic customs and traditions as the Irish chiefs virtually ignored the laws and regulations of the Dublin government.

Strategic considerations were among the main reasons for England's interest in its neighbor. Ireland held the key to the back door of England. The English feared that Catholic Ireland might make alliances with Catholic France and Spain, thus becoming a base for the invasion of England.

The key to any English policy was to bring a semblance of order to the chaos that existed. An account in the state papers for 1515 describes the confusing state of affairs in Ireland: "More than sixty counties called regions inhabited with the king's Irish enemies ... where reigneth more sixty captains wherein some call themselves kings, some princes, some Dukes, some Archdukes that liveth only by the sword and obeyeth unto no other temporal person ... and every of the said captains maketh war and peace for himself.... Also

27

there be thirty great captains of the English folk that follow the same Irish order and every of them maketh war and peace for himself without any license of the king."[17]

Henry's approach to solving England's Irish problem was to adopt a policy of surrender and regrant. He set about making agreements with individual chieftains, both Anglo-Irish and Gaelic, by which their lands were restored to them automatically under knight-service provided that certain conditions were met. They had to agree to recognize the supreme authority of the English Crown, to use English law, to observe English customs, and to disband private armies that did not receive the official sanction of the king's deputy in Ireland. As part of the deal, the Irish chieftains were given English titles. Thus Mourrouch O'Brien became the earl of Thormond and Donough O'Brien, the baron of Ibrakin. Con O'Neill, the great chieftain of Ulster, swore loyalty to the Crown in December 1541 and took the title of the earl of Tyrone. He had his eldest son recognized as successor rather than his other son or his nephews, who had more legitimate claims to earldom under Gaelic custom.

This proved to be the big flaw in the policy of surrender and regrant. The lands the Irish chiefs enjoyed during their lifetimes were not their personal property but belonged to the whole community. Land was actually allocated to the office of the chief and not to his person or family. Also, Irish law did not accept the English principle that a man should be succeeded by his eldest male heir. The successors of Irish chiefs were elected. Before too long, many Irish chiefs were challenging the king's grants. Thus when Conn O'Neill died in 1559, the earldom of Tyrone came under dispute. While the authorities in Dublin recognized Conn's illegitimate son Mathew as earl, the Irish in the earldom favored Shane O'Neill, a younger son. Shane dropped his English title and reverted back to Irish ways. Unable to defeat him in battle, the English invited Shane to London to negotiate. O'Neill returned triumphant to Ulster with the title of "Captain of Tyrone."

Henry VIII's son, Edward VI (1537–53), continued to extend

the Pale, waging war against Irish chiefs who tried to resist the English policy of surrender and regrant. During his reign the first effort to introduce loyal, reliable English subjects—a policy which became known as plantation—was first introduced. Settlers were brought to Counties Leix and Offaly, where they supplanted the natives. But this first try at plantation was unsuccessful. The cattle of the English settlers were driven off and their homes burned by the original occupants. During the reign of Queen Mary (1553–58), English settlers were again brought into Counties Leix and Offaly on condition that they employ only imported English labor. These settlements also failed to take root, but the plantation idea would not be abandoned.

During her long reign, the last Tudor monarch, Queen Elizabeth (1558–1603), stubbornly tried to introduce plantations in Munster and Leinster in the 1580s and twice in Ulster in the 1590s. A rebellion in Munster, first led by James Fitz Maurice Fitzgerald and then by his cousin the earl of Desmond, was crushed in 1580. Land totaling 400,000 acres was confiscated and divided into lots varying from 4,000 to 12,000 acres, which were to be allocated to "undertakers" who were to bring in English-born families. The whole management of this plantation proved to be incompetent and slow; the surveying was inaccurately done and it took years before the grantees took actual possession of the land. A commission of inquiry set up to investigate the plantation in 1592 found it a failure. Only 13 of the 48 undertakers had come to Ireland to live, and there were only 258 English families on the land. A few years later the Munster Plantation was swept away in the insurrection of 1598.

Elizabeth did not consider it realistic to try a wholesale settlement of English in the outlying Irish districts. The Irish were too numerous; Ireland was in too much a state of unrest. The country was not safe enough to attract a substantial number of English settlers. Those few who went to Ireland were attacked, harassed, and discouraged from staying. Elizabeth had to cope with numerous rebellions as the chiefs fiercely resisted the Tudor efforts at piecemeal conquest of Ireland and the suppression of the Gaelic way of life. But much of Connacht, Munster, and Leinster was brought under control; only Ulster continued to be a thorn in the side of the English government. A war against the stubborn northern province, the last major bastion of Gaelic tradition, was becoming an inevitable outcome of English policy. If Ireland was to be brought under control, then a final war of conquest would have to be waged against the heart of the resistance.

War did come, in 1592. For ten years the fighting was hard and brutal as the British poured money and men into Ulster. Under the bold and capable leadership of Hugh O'Neill, who had forged an alliance with his O'Donnell neighbors, the Ulster resistance was able to hold its own against superior enemy forces and impose a crushing defeat on the English at the Battle of Yellow Ford in 1598. This triggered a general uprising throughout Ireland, and the rebels sought help from Catholic Spain.

Elizabeth realized the dangerous situation and decided in April 1599 to send a massive army of 17,000 soldiers under the command of Sir Robert Devereux, the earl of Essex. Devereux made two brief expeditions against the Irish and then disobeyed Elizabeth's instructions when he made a truce with Hugh O'Neill, which lasted until the end of 1599. Devereux was recalled and rewarded for his effort with the ax in February of the following year.

Devereux's successor was Sir Charles Blount, Lord Mountjoy, who, unlike his predecessor, had a carefully-thought-out plan of action. Rather than let O'Neill dictate the terms of battle and engage the wily Ulster chieftain in skirmishes, Mountjoy concentrated on strengthening and building garrisons and carrying out a savage war of attrition, destroying cattle and crops and cutting off O'Neill from his source of supply. With Mountjoys's campaign succeeding, O'Neill turned to Spain for the aid that had been promised. Four thousand Spaniards landed in September 1601, not in Ulster where lay the strength of the resistance but in the south in Kinsale, County Cork, where the Irish had been all but subdued and where support for the northern chieftain O'Neill was lacking. Brilliantly outmaneuvering the enemy, O'Neill and his ally Hugh O'Donnell did manage to march the length of Ireland to Kinsale to make their stand. On Christmas Eve 1601 began what can now be seen as the final battle of survival for Gaelic Ireland. Fighting out in the open and not in the familiar Ulster bogs and marshes, O'Neill's forces were no match for the English. They were decisively routed and forced to flee north. Approximately 900 Scots were reported to have fought on the Irish side; 840 of them were slain. O'Donnell fled to Spain, only to die the next year. Hugh O'Neill managed to make it back to Ulster, where he led the life of a fugitive. On March 30, 1603, O'Neill formally surrendered to Mountjoy at Mellifont, County Louth. Ironically, the great Queen Elizabeth had died only six days before. Had Hugh O'Neill known, he might have negotiated a more honorable settlement with her successor, James I, whom he knew and with whom he had much in common.

2

The Ulster Plantation

Ever since the Norman king of England, Henry II, had first landed in Ireland in the latter part of the twelfth century, the English had been persistently but vainly trying to extend their authority over the entire island. Their biggest problem had been the stubborn resistance of the fiercely independent Irish chieftains of the north. Now, however, with the decisive defeat of Hugh O'Neill and his followers, Ulster finally lay open to English control.

The new English monarch, James I, moved quickly to take advantage of this golden opportunity to break the back of the old Gaelic order. Many of the garrisons that had played such important roles in the wars of the 1590s were maintained in the north to safeguard against any further outbreaks of trouble. English law was introduced, and those Irish customs that clashed with the new statutes were declared illegal. Sheriffs and justices of the peace were appointed. A system of counties on the English model was mapped out for the entire province of Ulster. Although peace was made with the belligerents, an important change occurred. O'Neill, Rory O'Donnell, and some of the lesser chiefs who had been involved in the rebellion had their lands restored to them, but now they were merely tenants-in-chief of the Crown. In addition, the proud O'Neill and O'Donnell had to swear fealty to James I.

The idea of planting the north with loyal and reliable English settlers, an idea abandoned during Queen Elizabeth's time, now seemed possible. The brutal campaigns waged in the north by the

English had caused widespread devastation, famine, and plague. Contemporary accounts give a very depressing picture of the north during the early seventeenth century. In 1610 one Englishman wrote, "Dispoyled, she present herself (as it were) in a sad, sabled robe, ragged (indeed) there remayneth nothing but ruynes and desolation, with a very little showe of humanities."[1] War had decimated the north's population and caused many people to flee to safer parts of Ireland.

Bright English officials put their minds to work to come up with workable plans to take advantage of the situation and strengthen the royal control of the north. In 1605, just two years after the cessation of hostilities, the lord deputy of Ireland, Sir Arthur Chichester, had proposed a scheme for the entire Ulster county of Cavan, in which settlers could be given land without dispossessing the native Irish. In the six counties, which were later forfeited to the Crown, it was estimated that the Irish could occupy one-third of the available land, while the other two-thirds could easily accommodate forty thousand English settlers. At first, James looked askance at any plan to sponsor a plantation in Ireland, but soon he became one of its most enthusiastic promoters, eventually believing that such a project was a noble undertaking for a monarch. At the same time, he shrewdly realized that a plantation would provide a great opportunity to enrich the royal coffers.

The Ulster Plantation took shape during an age when England was eagerly looking for new lands to colonize. In 1583 Sir Humphrey Gilbert had taken formal possession of Newfoundland. The East India Company, the great trading company, was organized in 1600, and seven years later Jamestown, the first permanent colony in America, was established. Although the New World offered opportunities for the mother country, many English leaders were convinced that Ireland was of much more importance to British interests. This was particularly true of the English privy-council and its solicitor-general Francis Bacon, who believed that the establishment of a strong base in the north of Ireland would protect England's flank and lead to the overall extension of English power. Chichester too was enthusiastic, and he wrote that he would "rather labour with his hands in the Plantation of Ulster than dance or play in that of Virginia."[2]

There was already evidence that settlers could be successfully planted in the north. For centuries Antrim and Down, the two counties closest to Scotland and, in many ways, an extension of the Scottish lowlands, had attracted a steady stream of Scottish settlers. The Scottish colony in this part of Ulster grew as a result of events in the early 1600s. Randal MacDonnell, in reward for his part in helping to subdue the Tyrone rebellion, was given a knighthood and a grant of land consisting of the north half of County Antrim, from Larne to Portrush. This substantially added to the holdings of the MacDonnells, who, as we have seen, already occupied the northeast part of the country. Although they were Catholic highlanders, they looked to the lowlands, a closer, more populated region, to bring over settlers to develop this acquisition. So successful was MacDonnell in his task that when he received the title of earl of Antrim in 1620, James specifically mentioned "his having strenuously exerted himself in settling British subjects on his estates."[3]

Two enterprising Scottish lairds from Ayrshire, Hugh Montgomery and James Hamilton, played a major role in establishing a colony in County Down. Con O'Neill, an Irish chieftain who had large landholdings in both Antrim and Down and who lived in an old mansion house of Castlereagh a few miles from Carrickfergus Castle, was having a party and ran out of wine. Con actually had wine, but it had been confiscated at Belfast by government officials because of his failure to pay the duty. Now very drunk, Con ordered some of the servants to go to Belfast and bring back the wine, using force if necessary. When his servants reached Belfast, they encountered some English soldiers. An argument ensued and led to a fight, resulting in one of the English soldiers being killed.

The English, who were hungrily eyeing Con's vast landownings, held the old chieftain responsible and accused him of "levying war against the queen."[4] It looked for a time as if Con's drunken indiscretion would cost him his head. His wife became desperate and sought the help of her Scottish friend Hugh Montgomery. Montgomery agreed to arrange for Con's escape in return for half of his land. He entrusted this task to a relative, Thomas Montgomery, the owner of a ship that occasionally made trips to Carrickfergus. Montgomery began by making love to the daughter of the keeper of Carrickfergus Castle. This gained him admittance to Con's room, where he gave the prisoner a large cheese on the pretext of bringing him food. Inside the cheese was a rope, which Con used to let himself out of the window to Montgomery's waiting ship and to safety in Scotland.

James Hamilton was brought into the deal to help secure O'Neill's pardon. The final agreement gave each lord a third of Con's property. King James ratified the agreement on the condition that "these lands should be planted with British Protestants, and that no grant should be made to any person of mere Irish extraction."[5]

Soon after, Hamilton and Hugh Montgomery returned to the Scottish lowland to recruit settlers. They were extremely successful, and before long there was a steady movement of people from the southwest of Scotland to Counties Antrim and Down. Once established, these settlers then persuaded friends and relatives to come; within ten years of the first settlement, an estimated eight thousand settlers resided in the two counties. They became the beachhead by which thousands of Scottish settlers made their way to the north of Ireland during the seventeenth century.

In addition to those Scottish efforts, there was one other important example of a plantation that was off to a successful start. For his contributions to the war effort, Sir Arthur Chichester received large tracts of land in 1603 in County Antrim. Chichester brought settlers from his own county of Devon and encouraged others from Cheshire and Lancashire to settle his lands. Chichester repaired the castle at Belfast and built a great house at Carrickfergus. His plantation proved to be very successful.

The great opportunity to introduce wholesale resettlement

came in 1607. The earls of Tyrone and Tyronnell had never really reconciled themselves to the defeat that the English had inflicted on them. They brooded about their loss of status, Irish titles, and political independence. No longer great kings but now mere landlords, they felt humiliated at being dependent on the goodwill of a foreign monarch. They watched helplessly as the British chipped away at their Gaelic way of life. And they grumbled about the amount of land the British had given them, the spread of English law, and the presence of foreign troops, which Tyrone called "shackles and handlocks" and "pricks in my side."[6]

The earls were suspicious too of English intentions. In 1606 a dispute arose between Tyrone and Donnell O'Cohan, a fellow Ulster chief to whose land Tyrone had made a claim. Both were summoned to London, where James was to adjudicate their quarrel. Meanwhile, a vague rumor began to circulate about an imminent Spanish invasion of Ireland. Tyrone was said to be in communication with the Spanish. Getting wind of the rumor and fearing arrest if he went to see James, Tyrone secretly boarded a ship in Lough Swilly on September 3, 1607, and fled to the Continent. Accompanying the two earls was the cream of the Irish aristocratic crop—friends, relatives, and followers—all leaving Ireland forever. This exodus, known as the Flight of the Earls, was a major landmark in Irish history. It left Ireland leaderless and its people helpless.

Although caught by surprise, the English quickly took advantage of the situation. The earls' sudden departure was taken as proof of their treachery against the Crown. The lands of the earls and their followers—the greater part of Ulster—was confiscated and declared forfeit to the Crown. In the same year, more land became available when a disgruntled Irish chieftain, Sir Cahir O'Doherty, the earl of Inishowen, unexpectedly staged a rebellion. Although managing to capture and burn Derry, he had little support outside of his own territory. His rebellion was quickly crushed, and he was killed. Counties Tyrone, Armagh, Cavan, Fermanagh, and Coleraine (later County Londonderry)—close to four million acres—now lay at the disposal of the British. The Irish-solicitor wrote that the king had in Ulster a greater extent of land "than any prince in Europe had to dispose of."[7]

Even before O'Doherty's rebellion, the government had begun to plan the settlement of the confiscated lands with English and Scottish settlers. A detailed plan of settlement was devised for County Tyrone, and the proposal was so well-liked by the government officials who studied it that the English privy council decided to apply the plan to the other five provinces. After much discussion, committee meetings, and surveys to determine how much of the available land should be included in the settlement, a final plan was drawn up in the spring of 1610.

Whereas the earlier culmination of Antrim and Down had been the result of private enterprise, the 1610 scheme represented a systematic exercise in government planning. The English wanted to ensure that a solid Protestant community planted by reliable settlers and working toward making the plantation a viable British colony would flourish. As the settlers arrived, they were to be neatly fitted into the plantation scheme. Land was given to three types of proprietors: English and Scottish undertakers, so called because of the conditions they undertook to fulfill; servitors (government officials and military officers and personnel), who were rewarded for their service to the Crown during the recent troubles; and what the English considered to be "deserving" Irish.

The undertakers and servitors were given allotments of 2,000, 1,500 and 1,000 acres, depending on their conditions of settlement. The most important figure in the plantation was the undertaker, who was required not only to live on the land himself but also to bring in a suitable number of settlers in proportion to the size of the grant, to house them in fortified villages, and to provide for their defense. No Irish were permitted to live on the undertakers' estates because the estates were expected to be self-contained British outposts in the new colony. Since many of the servitors had military experience and could protect themselves in case of trouble, they were allowed to keep Irish tenants on their land. Those undertakers and servitors receiving 2,000 acres were required to bring in a minimum of forty-eight Scottish or English tenants to settle on their estates.

Only a small number of the native Irish in each county were considered "deserving." For the most part, the land they received was situated in the least fertile regions of each county. Their estates were small, usually averaging between 100 and 300 acres. It is estimated that about 290 Irish grantees received land averaging from about 10 to 25 percent of the total acreage in each county. The plan also set aside land for the establishment of about four towns and one grammar school in each county, provided for the income of the Protestant clergy, and gave a substantial grant of land to the recently established Trinity College of Dublin. Monaghan was the only Ulster county not affected by the settlement plan.

One important exception was made to the system. All of County Coleraine, about one-tenth of the assigned land, was given to a consortium of business interests representing twelve great London companies. The companies accepted their grant with the undertakers' conditions, which included the exclusion of the Irish tenants from their lands. With some previous success in establishing the Jamestown colony, the consortium was eager to involve itself in other potentially profitable colonial enterprises. The group rebuilt the walls of Derry (recently damaged in the O'Doherty rebellion) and renamed the city of Derry as Londonderry and County Coleraine as County Londonderry. However, the consortium's failure to observe regulations concerning Irish tenants resulted in the confiscation of its Irish landholdings by the English authorities.

It was not until the plan was well along that the Scots were invited to participate. In 1609 King James sent a proclamation to the Scottish privy council announcing that those interested should apply directly to the council, whereupon the applicant would be given details of the plantation scheme. Seventy-eight applied as undertakers, of which only fifty-nine were finally selected to go to Ireland. When the final choice was made, Chichester's advice to include men of "rank and qualities" was heeded. Those selected were either nobles or knights, coming from within a twenty-five-mile radius of Edinburgh, the richest part of Scotland. A significant number of the undertakers came from the great families of Scotland: the earl of Abercorn and his brothers; the duke of Lennox; Sir Thomas Boyd; one of the sons of Lord Kilmarnock; and Lord O'Chiltree and his son. James thought that the influence of the powerful Scottish nobles would be so beneficial to the development of the plantation that he personally appealed to a number of them to participate. In addition, two Scots—Captains Patrick Crawford and William Stewart—were selected as servitors and settled in Donegal. They had been to Ulster before, bringing over approximately 200 Scots in 1608 to help put down O'Doherty's rebellion.

The Scots began to arrive in Ireland to look over their estates in August 1610. In all, forty-five appeared in person or sent Scottish agents to represent them. Some arrivers were truly impressed with what they saw. Sir John Davie, a poet and lawyer, said that an accurate description of the County Fermanagh landscape "would rather be taken for a poetical fiction than a true and serious narration."[9] But the Scots came to better themselves and not to admire the scenic beauty. Ulster was still feeling the effects of the savage conflict that had despoiled the land. One area between Donaghee in County Down and Newton in Armagh, for example, was described as a place in which "thirty cabins could not be found, nor any stone walls, but ruined, roofless churches, and a few vaults at Grey Abbey, and a stump of an old castle at Newton."[10] Some of the Scots reacted as did George Smailholm, a Leith resident, who took one look at his estate and returned to Scotland, refusing to have anything more to do with the plantation.

Settlement was slow. Within the first year, only about a third of the settlers required under the articles of the plantation had made it to Ulster. Many English officials were doubtful that the plantation could succeed. Comparing Ulster with Virginia, one government official wrote: "Our plantations go on, the one doubtfully, the other desperately. Ireland with all our money and pains is not yet settled in any fashion to assure us either profit or safety."[11] Some of the undertakers gave up easily when they saw that their expectations could not be met quickly. They were in the minority, however, and mainly from England. The Scots, on the whole, stuck with it, if only for a few years.

In 1611 the English privy council decided to investigate how much progress had been made in establishing the Ulster Plantation.[12] The council sent George Carew, a man well-qualified for the task. Between 1574 and 1603, he had spent twelve years in Ireland, either as a soldier or as an official in the Irish government. During the latter part of his stay he had risen to the presidency of Munster. Carew traveled with great speed across the north, talking with governors and sheriffs in each county. His survey provides a good indication of the extent of the Scottish migration during the first year of the plantation.

Out of fifty-nine undertakers, only forty-two had actually settled their estates or sent agents to occupy their land. An additional five were represented in the north by their servants. Only twenty-five had started to build anything of permanence. The historian M. Perceval-Maxwell estimated that there were "350 adults, including women, on the estates of the Scots, and there may have been twice that number."[13]

Worried that the plantation was not taking root, the English conducted another survey in 1612 under the direction of Sir Joshia Bodley, an administrator who had served the English Crown in England continuously since 1598. His survey indicated that Scottish migration was beginning to pick up, with the Scottish population at least doubling in the eighteen months since Carew's survey and perhaps increasing considerably more.[14]

Conditions in Scotland were encouraging migration to northern Ireland. Scotland was economically backward; the average Scot was poor and his life hard. Adding to his troubles was the introduction in 1610 of a new system of land tenure, called the *feu*, which dispossessed many of the Scottish farmers of their land and forced them to work as hired laborers. Thus, the thought of moving to Ireland and getting a new lease on life appealed to many. There they could find land that was much more fertile than at home. The farms were larger too, and they had the choice of doing what they wanted with their land. If life in Ulster did not live up to its promise, they could always come home. After all, it was just a short boat journey back to Scotland.

The lowland Scot, who was particularly affected by adverse economic conditions, was willing to try his luck in Ulster. Moreover, the move would not mean a complete break with his past, since contact with families and their hometowns could be easily maintained. Consequently, the flow of settlers from Scotland during the seventeenth century came not from the highlands but from the lowlands, the region nearest the English border. As the historian James Leyburn has so eloquently put it: "They were not clansmen who wore kilts and who marched, complete with dirk, sparren, brooch and bonnet, to the skirling of bagpipes in the glens. On the contrary, they were farmers who eked out a bare living on thin soil as a tenant or a laird."[15]

The Scots who had settled Ulster before 1603, such as the MacDonnells of the Glens, were Gaels like the Irish and had much in common with them. These Scots who came after the establishment of the plantation were Protestant in religion and spoke a different dialect of English. Galloway, the county closest to Ireland, provided the greatest number of settlers. The next-largest number came from Berwich and Lothins, the counties around Edinburgh. A smaller number came from the northwest in the area between Aberdeen and Inverness.

The tenants, whom the chief undertakers induced to go to Ireland, formed the backbone of the Scottish migration. Most came for the land, which the plantation gave them. Castles, bawns, and churches had to be constructed, and the sudden demands of the plantation building program could not be met by the local pool of tradesmen. Supplies were needed, and merchants found that a higher profit could be made in the struggling colony. One observer noted that an Englishman could become richer in four years in Ireland than in ten in England because the cost of necessities in the former were lower while the profit margins were the same.[16]

The Ulster Plantation, like other English colonies, attracted its share of undesirables. Some contemporaries were wholly unimpressed with the type of settler who came over during the early years. The Reverend Andrew Stewart, the minister of Donaghadee from 1645 to 1671, wrote: "And from Scotland came many, and from England not a few, yet all of them generally the scum of both nations, who, for debt, or breaking in fleeting from justice, or seeking shelter, came hither, hoping to do without fear of man's justice in a land where there was nothing, or but little, as yet, of the fear of God ... for their carriage made them to be abhorred at home in their native land, in so much that going to Ireland was looked upon as a miserable part of a deplorable person—yea, it was turned into a proverb, and one of the worst expressions of disdain that could be invented was to tell a man that Ireland would be his hinder end."[17]

Another Scottish minister, Robert Blair, reached the same conclusions about the new arrivals: "Although amongst those whom Divine Providence did send to Ireland, there were several persons eminent by birth, education, and parts; yet the most part were such as either poverty, scandalous lives, or at the best, adventurous seeking of better accommodation had forced thither, so that the security and thriving of religion was little seen to by those adventurers, and to preachers were generally of the same complexion."[18]

It was difficult for the authorities to control the movement of people and goods between Ireland and Scotland. Wanted criminals fled to the plantation, knowing that the authorities would seldom make an effort to track them down. The trade in stolen goods flourished. Livestock, in particular, was in great demand, and few settlers cared where it came from as long as the price was right. The authorities tried to introduce measures to control the illicit trade. One plan called for the establishment of a ferry system that would funnel all trade through specific and supervised ports. This, however, met with little success.

As the planters migrated from England and Scotland to begin their new life, a distinctive settlement pattern took shape. The Scots settled mainly in the northern and eastern parts of Ulster, where they predominated, while the English tended to concentrate in the southern part of the province. Of the six plantation counties, Donegal and Tyrone were given almost wholly to the Scots, Armagh and Derry were prevailingly English, and Fermanagh and Cavan showed both Scottish and English influence.

The move to northern Ireland was fraught with dangers. Just the mere task of crossing the few miles of sea between Scotland and Ireland could be risky. The settler had to face storms and other natural calamities, as well as the possibility of attack by pirates hiding among the many islands and inlets of Ireland's east coast. In a letter from Dublin Castle dated June 27, 1610, Chichester wrote: "The pirates upon this coast are so many and are becoming as bold that now they can come into this channel, and have lately robbed divers boats, both English and Scotch, and have killed some that have made resistance. They lay for the landowner's money sent for the work at Coleraine, but missed it; they bread a great terror to all passengers, and me thinks will not spare the treasure if they may light upon it."[19]

Ships themselves were often leaky and in poor condition, and there was no guarantee that they could make it across the channel. When Scottish settlers arrived, they found that their estates were often situated in the more barren parts of the province. One tenant complained that he often had to carry his timber from as far away as twenty-two miles, while the stone for the building had to be hauled twelve miles "over filthie boggie montanes.[20] The wolf proved to be a great danger to the settlements, killing many cattle and causing the authorities to spend much time in trying to track down the predator. The menace proved so great that as late as 1652, the English government was offering a bounty of six pounds for the head of every female wolf.

Adding to the settler's problems was the ever-present danger of an Irish rebellion. The Irish came to hate the planters, who they believed had stolen their land. The Irish had much to feel resentful about. From the first, they were miserably treated. Allowed no say in the government of the plantation, they were regarded as second-class citizens, contemptuously called the "mere Irish" by the settlers. They were constantly under pressure to change their customs and way of life. Even those who had been given land under the conditions of the plantation did not fare too well. Their holdings were often located in the more infertile and mountainous parts of Ulster, and they had to struggle to eke out a meager existence.

The settlers were constantly on the alert, living with the fear that the more numerous Irish would rise up and slaughter them. Their fears seemed justified when, in 1615, just a few years after the first settlers began coming over, a plot to overthrow the plantation was uncovered. In the making for three years, it called for an attack on the main centers of settlement, the release of the earl of Tyrone's bastard son who was imprisoned at Charlemont, the capture of the most important plantation officials, and the killing of the rest. The government knew of the badly planned plot long before it could be put into operation, however. Arrests were made, and several of the leaders were sentenced and executed.

Many of the Irish who were unwilling to live as tenants on the land they had once owned fled to hills and bogs to live as outlaws, looking for opportunities to strike back against the British. They were joined by the soldiers of O'Neill and O'Donnell, for whom no provision had been made after the earls had left for the Continent. Realizing the danger that these swordsmen posed, Chichester had a number of them shipped to Sweden to serve in the armies of King Charles IX. But many of them eluded capture. They became known as "woodkernes" and then "tories," a term used later to refer to a British political party.

The settlers feared these men of the mountains and bogs. Not strong enough to fight traditional methods of warfare, the woodkernes reverted to guerrilla tactics, living by plundering the countryside and conducting sneak attacks on the settlements. The outlaw existence became a way of life for many of the native Irish. In a government report of March 27, 1624, one official commented on the robberies and attacks being committed by bands operating in Counties Londonderry and Tyrone and added, "I know well that this is a trifle to speak of in this kingdom, where such causes have been frequent, and where there are now many others in several counties."[21]

The English authorities adopted ruthless measures to deal with this serious threat to the plantation. Tough laws were enacted, making it a crime to aid and abet the outlaws. So seriously were the woodkernes taken that one English undertaker, Thomas Clenerhasset, suggested in a pamphlet written in 1610 that the settlers should organize manhunts to track them down. "No doubt it will make a pleasant hunt," he wrote, "and much prey will fall to the followers."[22] His suggestion was soon followed, and bloodhounds were used in the hunt.

If caught, the woodkerne was often shot without a trial. When tried, he was more than likely found guilty. After sentencing, the unfortunate captive had a halter placed around his neck and was paraded through the streets of the town to his place of execution, where he was hanged. Not too successful in controlling the menace, the English seriously considered the establishment of a permanent force in England and Scotland, ready to go to Ireland at the first hint of trouble.

If the settler felt insecure in his new environment, so also did the English authorities about the chances that the plantation would succeed. Much evidence indicated that the plantation was not worth the investment. The English soon realized that the plantation had not done as well as they had hoped. One of the main reasons was that the maps on which the land was granted to the settlers were seriously deficient. The plantation grantees, including the London companies, received much larger proportions than they should actually have received. This meant much smaller rent revenues for the government. Realizing the error, the English talked about having the entire plantation resurveyed, but nothing was ever done.

In addition, many of the undertakers lacked the means to carry out the requirements of the plantation. They did not erect the castles or fortify the houses as required and had great difficulty in bringing over the required number of English and Scottish settlers. Many of those settlers who did come eventually became discouraged, and some returned home. It is estimated that as many as half of the original settlers sold their estates and opted out of the enterprise. Furthermore, disputes arose between landlords and tenants over a host of problems.

The plantation failed to develop as planned in one other important respect. The English authorities had tried, in each of the six counties, to move the Irish from the lands given to the chief undertakers and transfer them to the lands of the servitors, the deserving Irish, and the churches. But many of the undertakers found it more profitable to keep the natives as tenants than to bring in British or Scottish colonists. The natives, unlike the settlers, were willing to pay higher rents and proved valuable as food producers and as a source of cheap labor. The government tried to enforce the regulations of the plantation. In 1618, for example, an attempt was made to levy fines on the native Irish living on undertaker lands, but many of the fines incurred were actually paid by the undertakers. Later, in 1622, a report based on a survey of the plantation denounced the undertakers in such strong terms that James seriously considered replacing all undertakers with others who could be relied on to "offer themselves punctual to perform all the covenants and conditions to the first plantation."[23] However, James vacillated and missed what might have been a golden opportunity to put the plantation back on a good footing.

By 1613, reports from the plantation were improving and showed that some progress was being mad in settling tenants and erecting the prescribed buildings. Despite the problems and the slow start, the period from 1613 to 1619 saw a steady movement of Scottish settlers to northern Ireland. One of the main catalysts to development was the pressure that James began to put on the undertakers to make them conform to the articles of the plantation. He was displeased with the findings of still another survey, conducted in 1614. In a letter to Chichester in 1615, James stated his intentions "to seize into our hands the lands of any man whatsoever, with respect of personnes, whether he be a British Undertaker Servitor or native, that shall be found defective in performing any of the articles of the plantation."[24] James decided to set an example; so, in 1616, he gave the earl of Abercarn a grant of all lands that had been forfeited by the undertakers in Strabane. Those undertakers had received land but had failed to fulfill the requirements of the grant. James thus hoped to frighten other undertakers into submission. This was the toughest measure taken by James toward the planters during his reign.

A major reason the plantation was strengthened during this period was the continuous replacement of unsuccessful undertakers with more capable ones. By 1619 only eighteen of the original undertakers or their wives still held their allotments. As landholders changed, so too did the size of the estates. The smaller landlords were bought out while the wealthier undertakers added to their holdings. Every county had examples of undertakers who added to their estates in the hope that greater revenues would result from their investment. In certain districts this expansion had the blessing of King James, who hoped that planters with more land in their possession would have a greater opportunity to make their settlements a success.

By the 1620s, the Scots who had come over were proving themselves important to the plantation scheme, although Scottish settlement was not as great as had been expected. A survey conducted in 1622 reported the Scottish adult male population at between 6,000 and 7,000. Of the original 81,000 acres received by the Scottish settlers, only 22,000 had been planted. But as the seventeenth century progressed, the Scots continued to come over in large numbers until, as the historian A. T. A. Stewart has noted, "the Scots eventually occupied an area of the plantation all out of proportion to that originally allotted to them."[25] Although figures on the Scottish immigration to the plantation vary considerably and are almost impossible to calculate accurately, it is estimated that by 1633, at least one-half and possibly two-thirds of all planters were Scots.[26] With the advantage of the short crossing from Scotland, many Scots were quick to see that the plantation offered them greater opportunities than they could find at home. When they arrived, their character, shaped by the bleak economic circumstances at home, helped them to get established in their new and, for the most part, hostile environment. They proved stubborn, tough, resilient, and hardworking—the same qualities their descendants later exhibited in America when the next great Scotch-Irish migration was made, in the eighteenth century. They built towns, villages, churches, and schools, cleared the land, drained the marshes and enclosed the fields, raised farm horses, and established homesteads.

Although the English too made important contributions to the establishment of the plantation, many contemporaries observed how their background and temperament did not suit them well in their attempts to deal with the hardships and dangers in Ulster. This was the belief of the Reverend Andrew Stewart: "It is to be observed that being a great deal more tenderly bred at home in England and entertained in better quarters than they could find there in Ireland, they were very unwilling to flock hither, except to good lands, such as they had before at home, or to good cities where they might trade; both of which in those days were scarce enough here. Besides that, the marshiness and fogginess of this Island was still found unwholesome to English bodies, more tenderly bred and in a better air; so that we have seen in our time multitudes of them die of a flux, called here the country disease, at their first entry."[27]

Many accounts, on the other hand, describe the Scottish settlements favorably and show that the Scots were slowly becoming the backbone of the plantation. The survey of 1619 concluded, "Were it not that the Scottish colonists carried on arable farming in many places, the country would be liable to starvation."[28] The commissioners, in their 1622 survey, said that the Scottish inhabitants of Strabane "were industrious and due daily benefice ... their Towne with new Buildings, strong and defensible."[29] Even in the very

English settled county of Londonderry, a Scottish settlement headed by a man named McClellan was regarded as the most established and best able to defend itself. Out of six Ulster counties included in the government's plantation scheme, Fermanagh was the only county in which Scottish settlement failed to take root. By 1619, according to the Pynnais survey, most of the Scottish estates had been sold to Englishmen.

By the time King James died in 1625, Antrim, Down, and the six escheated counties had about eight thousand Scotsmen capable of bearing arms for the Crown. Queen Elizabeth had spent great sums of money to establish an English military preserve in the north but had failed. England now had a formidable fighting force at practically no cost. As time passed, moreover, the planters became strong supporters of England and its interests. It looked as if the north of Ireland, which had seen so much warfare, was now set to embark on a period of peace and growth. The lord deputy of Ireland wrote in 1624, "Since Ireland was Ireland never was [there] such universal tranquility as at this moment."[30]

This appearance of tranquillity was deceiving, however; in actuality, the plantation of Ulster was built on very weak foundations. James' plantation scheme had created two mutually hostile and very separate cultures in the north, each with their own distinct language, laws, customs, and lifestyles. Most significant was religion, which proved to be the biggest difference between the Irish and the migrating Scots and English. The settlers were Protestant whereas the native Irish were Catholic. The Irishman's Catholicism stamped him with a mark of inferiority and was the main reason for his mistreatment. Each culture was distinct and went its own separate way. The Protestant colonists occupied the river farmlands while the Catholics were forced to scratch out a meager existence in the poorer, mountainous areas of Ulster. A revolt was inevitable, and it came with the great rebellion in 1641, when the whole system was swept aside.

3

Scotch-Irish Presbyterianism Takes Root in the Seventeenth Century

The settlers who came to Ireland from Scotland early in the seventeenth century to make a new life brought their Presbyterian religion with them. Under the fiery leadership of John Knox, the foundations for the Scottish Presbyterian Church were laid almost a half century before the beginning of the Ulster Plantation. Born in 1515, Knox has been described as a "dour, passionate, devout but remorseless reformer."[1] For much of his adult life, he relentlessly attacked the abuses of the Roman Catholic Church, which he considered an instrument of the devil.

Although church corruption was widespread all over Europe, many contemporaries believed it to be even worse in Scotland. By 1650, it was estimated that the property of the Scottish Catholic Church amounted to more than a third of all property in the country and half its wealth. The historian James Leyburn, in writing about the Catholic Church of this period, noted: "She was grasping of lands, of heritage, of influence. Abbeys were flourishing while religion was at a low ebb. Cathedrals and other establishments were rich, and prosperous churchmen walked among people who were poor, distressed and burdened."[2]

Accounts of the day describe the priests of the Scottish

Catholic Church as being greedy, uncouth, and even illiterate. Many could stumble through the words of the mass with only the greatest of difficulty. A wide segment of the Scottish people had lost all respect for the Catholic clergy and derisively and openly called them "dumb dogs" and "idle bellies." The corruption of the church was not limited to just the priesthood. In his report to Pope Paul IV in 1556, Cardinal Sermmeta stated that the "nuns in Scotland had come to such a pass of boldness that they utterly condemn the safeguards of chastity."[3]

The time was ripe for change. The movement for the reformation of the Scottish church gained momentum in 1559 when Knox returned from exile. Scotland was a keg of dynamite ready to explode. Just a short time before Knox's arrival, a document had been posted on the gates of every religious establishment in Scotland. It became known as the Beggar's Summons, a manifesto championing the poor and helpless and calling for the reform of ecclesiastical abuses. When Knox gave one of his impassioned speeches at Perth, a riot broke out. The parishioners destroyed all the religious statues in the church and then went on a rampage, doing the same thing to the other churches and religious houses in town.

A civil war erupted. The Queen-Regent, Mary of Guise, appealed to her daughter's husband, the French King, France II, for help. The Protestants in turn mustered an army and got the backing of Queen Elizabeth. The fighting lasted for a year; in the end, the French were forced to withdraw their troops from Scotland. On June 6, 1560, the Treaty of Leith was signed, solidifying the Protestant victory and putting an end to the church of Rome as the national church of Scotland. In its place, the Presbyterian Church became the established kirk of Scotland. A confession of faith was established, and several ministers prepared the First Book of Discipline, which provided for the governance of the church. On December 20, 1560, the first General Assembly of the Reformed Church was held in Edinburgh. Leaders of the Scottish Reformation attended, including Knox and fifteen other ministers.

3. Scotch-Irish Presbyterianism Takes Root

During the 1560s, John Knox worked hard to strengthen the new church; however, it was not too long after his death in 1572 that the Scottish king, James VI, attempted to establish an Episcopal-style church in Scotland. Stiff opposition arose to James' policies, and it was not until his succession to the English throne in 1603 as James I that he was able to get his way. He threw many Scottish church leaders in jail, abolished the general assembly, and set up an Episcopal form of church government.

The Presbyterian ministers who could not endure what they considered to be a "reversion to Papacy" left Scotland and sought refuge in the north of Ireland. Many of their parishioners followed. Because of the devastation caused by a decade of continuous war in Ulster, religion there, like most everything else in the province, was in a sorry state. The few churches still standing were generally in a dilapidated condition; tithes were not paid, and many of the parishes lacked clergy. In 1604 Sir John Davie wrote: "The churches are ruined and fallen down to the ground in all parts of the kingdom. There is no divine service, no christening of children, no receiving the sacrament, no Christian meeting or assembly, no, not once in a year; in a word no more demonstration of religion than amongst Tartaars or cannibals."[4]

As late as 1622, a royal commission reported that in the diocese of Down and Antrim alone, only 16 churches were fit for services while 150 churches and chapels had been destroyed or were in ruins. In the entire north, there were only 380 Protestant ministers for nearly 2,500 parishes.

The Episcopal Church had made little headway in Ireland during the sixteenth century, and so it was trying to get a foothold in Ulster at the same time that the Presbyterian ministers were arriving from Scotland. With no strong, established church to tell them what to do, the Scottish Presbyterians were free to practice their religion without fear of persecution.

Many of the Episcopalian bishops in Ireland held religious views similar to those of the incoming Presbyterians. Like the Scots, these bishops were Puritans and believers in Calvinist theology.

Since many of the parishes in the colony were without ministers, they allowed the Scottish ministers to join and preach within the pale of the Church of Ireland. The discipline of the established church was very weak; there was no rigid insistence that the Scots conform to its tenants. One bishop named Andrew Knox, for example, continued throughout his entire life to permit candidates during the ordination ceremony to omit those passages in the prayer book with which their consciences found fault. Thus, for some twenty years after the establishment of the Ulster Plantation, there was no religious persecution, and there were no separate Episcopal and Presbyterian Churches. The Irish Protestant Church was one and undivided.

The first Presbyterian ministers who came over during the formative years of the plantation were well educated and included some impressive and distinguished clergymen. Some had met with persecution at home and fled to Ireland in the hope that there they would find greater freedom to preach the gospel. Edward Brice is the first minister for whom there is any record. In 1607, Brice fiercely opposed the motion to make Archbishop Spottiswoode the permanent moderator of the Synod of Clydshire. Shortly afterward, he was forced to flee Scotland when faced with a trumped-up charge of adultery. Brice settled in Broadisland (or Ballycarry) in 1613. Although admitted to the Episcopal Church, he preached the Presbyterian doctrine and conducted his services in the Presbyterian manner.

One of the most renowned of the first group of Presbyterian ministers to come to Ireland was Robert Blair, a man described by one contemporary as having "a majestic appearance, deep piety, great learning and persuasive eloquence."[5] Blair resigned his position as professor at Glasgow University rather than submit to the policies that King James was trying to impose on the Scottish church. He was invited by James Hamilton to Bangor in 1623 and was ordained as one of Hamilton's vicars.

Other ministers followed, including Josiah Welsh, grandson of John Knox, in 1621, who was ordained a minister at Templepatrick by his relative Bishop Knox of Raphoe, and George Dunbar, who preached first at Carrickfergus and then later at Ballymena and Larne. Another was John Livingstone, the guardian of Mary Queen of Scots. He was considered one of the ablest linguists of his day, having a knowledge of eight languages including Chaldaic, Hebrew, and Greek. Soon after their arrival these ministers, along with others, built churches and introduced in their parishes the forms, practices, and disciplines of the Scottish Presbyterian Church. Helping to spread the faith throughout the plantation was the establishment of a monthly meeting place in County Antrim in 1626. At the meeting, which was held on the first Friday of each month, sermons were preached in the morning and afternoon. At night the ministers discussed and organized the affairs of the church. Throughout the plantation, the thirst for spiritual guidance and comfort was strong, and like their fellow Presbyterians in Scotland, the Scotch-Irish were eager to hear the preaching of the word of God and to receive instruction. The Reverend John Livingstone observed in 1630:

> I have known them to come several miles from their own houses to communion, to the Saturday sermon, and spending the whole Saturday's night in several companies, sometimes a minister being with them, and sometimes themselves alone in conference and prayer. They have then waited on the public ordinance the whole Sabbath and spend the Sabbath night in the same way and yet at the Monday's sermon were not troubled with sleepiness; and so they had not slept til they went home. In those days, it was no great difficulty for a minister to preach in public or private, such was the hunger of the hearers."[6]

After James' death in 1625, however, the period of religious tolerance in the British Isles and in Ireland gradually came to an end. Charles I, who succeeded James to the throne, shared his father's ardent belief in the divine right of kings and an intense hatred of Puritans. In 1628, William Laud became Charles' chief

agent in his attempt to force the Puritans to conform to the ortho-
dox practices of the Episcopal Church. When he assumed the position of bishop of London, Laud became a leader of a party that grew
in power in the Church of England—a party that regarded puri-
tanism as a danger not only to the church but also to the king. Laud
was determined to use any means at his disposal to thoroughly crush
nonconformism. Persecution in the British Isles intensified in 1633
when he became archbishop of Canterbury.

In Ireland too, particularly in the north, English officials were
alarmed at the state of religious nonconformity. In 1633, Robert
Echelin, the bishop of Down, suspended Robert Blair and John
Livingstone from their monasteries. The two appealed to
Archibishop James Ussher, who subsequently revoked their sus-
pension. Echelin then sent an agent to London and, with the help
of Laud, persuaded the king to agree that the two Presbyterian ministers be "tried as fanatic disturbers of the peace."[7] The ministers,
along with the other two notable ministers described earlier, George
Dunbar and Josiah Welsh, were asked to swear that they would
conform to Episcopacy. All four refused and were suspended.

To carry out his policies in Ireland, Laud appointed his friend
Thomas Wentworth (later earl of Strafford) as Lord Deputy of Ireland. In his defense it must be said that from his arrival in Ireland,
Wentworth ruled the country more efficiently than had ever been
done before, reforming the worst abuses in both the church and the
state. Under his able administration, industrialization was fostered,
churches were rebuilt, trade was improved, the burden of debt was
decreased, and ecclesiastical revenues were increased. Like Laud,
Wentworth was a great believer in the absolute power of the monarchy. By making Ireland prosperous, he hoped to yield additional revenue and resource for the Crown and make it stronger. In 1634 he
organized a new parliament, which gave him sweeping powers to
review land grants. He helped fill the royal coffers by fining the
London companies a total of £70,000 for nonfulfillment of conditions. By 1636 the Irish treasury had a surplus of accounts totaling
£50,000.

Wentworth's arrival and subsequent policies led to hard times for the Scotch-Irish Presbyterian settlers in the north. Ironically, only a few years before, these colonists had been seen as the bulwarks of English authority in Ireland. But the lord deputy, believing that nonconformity within the Irish Episcopal Church was a threat to the monarchy, ordered the bishops to enforce the Act of Uniformity in their dioceses. Wentworth did not trust the Scots and tried to discourage further emigration from Scotland. He even considered driving them out of the country. Wentworth's policies set the general tone for the English government's treatment of the Scotch-Irish settlements for most of the rest of the seventeenth century. As Leyburn says, "From 1634 to 1690, ... life for the colonists in Ulster was to consist of a series of crises some of them so prolonged and severe that the very existence of the Scottish settlement was threatened."[8]

Some of the Presbyterian ministers, refusing to put up with the new attitude of the established Irish Protestant Church, decided to leave Ireland and make a daring voyage across the Atlantic Ocean to a new life in New England. This was a little over eighty years before the first great wave of Scotch-Irish emigration to the New World began. A ship weighing 150 tons and christened the *Eagle Wing* was built near Belfast. On September 9, 1636, 140 people, including Robert Blair and three other ministers, boarded the ship and set sail from Belfast Lough. Strong winds, however, forced their return. On the second try, the *Eagle Wing* managed to make it halfway across the Atlantic before fierce storms caused extensive damage and forced it to limp back into Belfast Lough in November.

After the ship returned, Wentworth ordered the arrest of Blair and his fellow ministers, but they managed to flee to Scotland. Soon, other Presbyterian ministers did likewise as Wentworth replaced all Puritan-leaning bishops with his own men and ordered the new bishops to step up the pressure to force the Presbyterian ministers to conform to the practices of the Church of England.

For five years after 1636, most Scotch-Irish congregations were without their ministers. Many of the Presbyterian faithful were forced to make the journey across the North Channel to Scotland to take communion or have their children baptized. On one occasion as many as five hundred crossed over to celebrate the Lord's Supper at Stranraer under the exiled Livingstone. Those Presbyterian ministers who did remain in Ireland held secret services at night. Others pretended to be reformed but made a travesty of the regulations. Bishop Leslie of Raphoe complained that the Presbyterian ministers chopped down the liturgy to the lessons and a few short prayers and that, during the reading of these, the congregations walked about in the churchyard, rushing back into the church only when the sermon began.[9]

Laud's zealous attempt to impose ecclesiastical reforms extended to Scotland as well; however, when he ordered that the liturgy introduced by John Knox be replaced by a new High Church form comparable to the Anglican Book of Common Prayer, he seriously misjudged Scotland's loyalty to the Episcopal system. On July 23, 1637, he directed that the new liturgy ("Laud's Liturgy," as it became known) be read in the churches of Scotland. When the dean of Edinburgh attempted to read it in St. Giles Cathedral, an elderly woman named Janet Geddes picked up the stool upon which she was sitting, hurled it at the dean, and shouted, "Out, thou false thief, dost thou say mass at my lug [ear]."[10] An uproar ensued. People began shouting that popery was being brought back to Scotland. The service ended abruptly. All over Scotland, determined resistance arose to the new liturgy. Laud had set loose a chain of events that created the second Scottish Reformation and eventually led to King Charles' downfall. In March 1638, a National Covenant was drawn up and published, reaffirming the reforms instituted by John Knox. Copies were sent to Ulster and were signed by Presbyterian ministers and their congregations.

Although Laud's schemes to restore Episcopacy in Scotland failed, his agent Wentworth was determined that there would be more success in Ireland. He ordered all Ulster Scots over sixteen years of age to renounce the National Covenant and swear to what became known as the "Black Oath." Those who did not were to be punished severely. Some Presbyterians conformed, but the vast majority did not. Many of the latter were imprisoned and given heavy fines.

The severity of the fines can be illustrated through the fate of one Scotch-Irish man named Henry Stewart. He, his wife, their two daughters, and a servant were arrested, taken to Dublin, and tried in court. Stewart and his wife were each fined £5,000, while the other three were given fines of £2,000 each, for a total of £16,000. The party was to be kept in prison until the fine was paid. The severity of such fines and Wentworth's policies led to a surge in the Presbyterian exodus to Scotland. Ironically, this persecution helped save the Scotch-Irish from a possibly worse fate later in 1641, when the native Irish broke out in rebellion against the Protestants.

As relations between Scotland and King Charles worsened, the power of Wentworth, who was now earl of Strafford, continued to decline. When Wentworth learned of Charles' plans to invade Scotland in 1640, he raised an army of nine thousand men to help the king. The majority of the army, however, were Catholics. This was totally unacceptable to the increasingly powerful parliamentary party in England. Wentworth's enemies were eventually able to muster enough strength to have him recalled to England, where he was executed on May 12, 1641.

Meanwhile, the civil unrest in the British Isles encouraged the Catholic Irish to organize and plot the overthrow of their hated English overlords. Exiled Irishmen had been in contact with their relatives and fellow Catholics at home, preparing plans that they hoped would spark a general uprising, drive all foreigners out of the country, and make Ireland once again truly Gaelic. The plot was to begin on October 23, 1641, with a bold attempt to capture Dublin Castle, the very center of colonial power. Once Dublin was captured, the rebels planned to seize and arm themselves with the guns stored at the city's arsenal as a result of the demobilization of Wentworth's army. Such action, it was hoped, would encourage the native Irish to rise up, since they would be overjoyed at the prospect of regaining their lands and rights. At the very last moment, however, the plot was betrayed.

Although the conspirators called off the attack on the castle, rebellion broke out; however, it was confined mainly to the north, where the feeling of injustice and grievance was strongest among natives. The northern rebels were led by Sir Phelim O'Neill and Sir Conn Magennis of Inveagh, who, within a week, were successful in capturing much of Ulster with the exception of Donegal and Antrim. The rebels were able to seize important towns and strongholds, but the loyalists did manage to hold on to some key places, most notably Enniskillen, Derry, and Carrickfergus.

At first, the Scottish colonists did not suffer as much as the English, who were largely blamed by the natives for their troubles and whose settlements lay in the area that first came under attack. There is even evidence that the Scots were purposely left alone by the rebels. In a report presented to the House of Commons in July 1642, Colonel Audeley Mervyn stated, "In the infancy of the Rebellion the rebels made open proclamations, upon pain of death, that no Scotchman should be stirred in body, goods or lands, and that they should to this purpose write over the lyntels of their doors that they were Scotchman, and destruction might pass over their families."[11] Other, perhaps more important reasons why the Scottish Presbyterians did not feel the full fury of the rebel onslaught were that Wentworth had been sent to the gallows and that not enough time had elapsed to allow the Scots to return to Ireland. Ironically, religious persecution saved many Scottish lives.

Even to this day, controversy exists about how many people died during the initial stages of the rebellion. There are many accounts of the alleged atrocities committed by the rebels against the Protestant population. Much of the evidence is preserved at Trinity College in thirty-two bound volumes containing sworn statements of Protestants who supposedly experienced the events of 1641 firsthand. They tell of tortures, murders, forced drownings, burned houses, and other outrages. Some of the evidence can be considered suspect, since the statements were taken down by the royal commissioners a long time after the events allegedly occurred. Some of the evidence is hearsay, and a certain amount can by dismissed as exaggeration or outright lies. It does seem probable, however, that atrocities did occur. Ever since the establishment of the Ulster Plantation, many rebels had been forced to live as fugitives, hiding in the bogs and woods and trying to evade the English authorities who hunted them down like wild animals. Many of their comrades had been forced into the humiliating position of working as tenants on the land they had once owned. It seems likely that the rebels would not miss their chance to get even, to play the hunter instead of the hunted. While the actual number of people died will never be known, estimates have been put as high as 12,000.

To this day the events of 1641 have profound meaning for the Irish Protestants in the north. There has always been a fear of another Catholic uprising against an unprepared Protestant population. This has resulted in what historians have called a "seige mentality"—a belief that the Protestants of Northern Ireland must always be on guard against the Catholics, who cannot really be trusted. One scene well illustrates this state of mind. Each July 12, Protestants march through the streets of Belfast to celebrate the victory of Protestant King William of Orange over the Catholic King James II at the Boyne River in 1690. One banner is held high, keeping the memory of 1641 very much alive. It depicts the events on a bridge at Portadown in County Antrim on a cold day in November 1641. An estimated one hundred Protestants were stripped naked, driven from their houses, and then forced to jump from the bridge to the cold water below. Many drowned; others tried to climb to shore but were clubbed to death for their troubles.

The eleven years of warfare that followed the rebellion were immensely complicated. Several groups—Scots, Ulster colonists, English royalists, English parliamentarians, the Anglo-Irish, the native Irish, and even the Papacy—became involved in a bewildering array of shifting loyalties and allegiances. The English Parliament immediately voted to send an army to Ireland to deal with the crisis, but because of financial problems, a plan had to be devised to raise money. The Adventurers Act, passed by Parliament in 1642, proclaimed that all land owned by the rebels would be declared forfeit when the rebellion was quashed. Two and a half million acres of land were sold for a total of one million pounds to speculators and to those who promised to fight in Ireland. Since the adventurers needed some guarantee that their investment would be honored, one clause in the law forbade any clemency to the rebels. Most of the money raised, however, would be used by Parliament to finance its war with King Charles I.

An agreement was reached between the Irish and Scottish Parliaments whereby a detachment of twenty-five hundred Scottish troops under the command of Major General Robert Munro was sent to Ireland to protect the country's Protestants. The troops arrived in Carrickfergus in April 1646. Munro was made commander-in-chief of all parliamentary forces in Ireland. In the meantime, the Catholic Confederacy was established in May at Kilkenny. Its aim was "to defend religion and the king against sectaries and establish the Catholic religion as full as at any time since Henry VII."

In June, Munro took the offensive, defeating the Catholic forces in the north and recapturing Dungannon, Newry, and Mountjoy. Munro's initial military successes gave Parliament a foothold in Ireland. At this stage of the conflict, Protestant settlers in the north were divided in their loyalties, with some supporting King Charles I and others backing Parliament. Had it not been for the presence of Munro's Scottish troops, it appears most likely that many of the British in Ulster would have declared for the king. It also seems probable that Dublin, the other main center of Protestant resistance to Ireland, would not have held out alone. As one historian has concluded, "Ireland might have fallen into the hands of the confederates, with consequences for the future of the British Isles as a whole which are incalculable."[13]

With peace established over a large part of Ulster, the opportunity lay open to firmly establish the Presbyterian Church in Ulster. The rebellion had literally swept away the Episcopal

Church, and most of Ulster lacked any semblance of church organization. The chaplains in the Scottish army were ordained ministers of the Church of Scotland; many of Munro's officers were elders. After four kirk sessions were formed in the army, it was decided to form a presbytery. The first meeting was held at Carrickfergus on June 10, 1642. Five chaplains and an elder from each of the four regimental sessions attended. After receiving applications from various places in Ulster, the presbytery sent ministers to the most promising. Elderships were created at several towns in Counties Antrim and Down.

As a result, according to the church historian George Reid, "the foundations of the Presbyterian church were once more laid in Ulster, in exact conformity with the parent establishment in Scotland." So solid were these foundations, wrote another historian, T. W. Moody, that the Presbyterian Church "was able to maintain itself against all subsequent efforts of the established church to have it suppressed."[14]

The newly formed Irish Presbyterian Church helped to strengthen the beleaguered Protestant colony. Many of the Scots who had fled Ireland just a few years earlier began to return and helped to make the church grow. During the 1640s other Scots fled the civil war in Scotland and crossed the channel to Ireland, thus adding to the Presbyterian population. A large number of Presbyterians from England sought refuge in northern Ireland too, to escape the persecution of Charles I. Although many Scottish Presbyterians lost their lives in the fighting, the colony was also strengthened by the fact that many of Munro's men settled in Ireland. By 1648, just five years after the establishment of the first presbytery and with the fighting still raging, more than twenty congregations in the north had permanent pastors.

The situation in Ireland was complicated by the outbreak of civil war in England in August 1642. While the Protestant Parliament in Dublin was divided in loyalty between King Charles I and the English Parliament, the Catholic Confederacy at Kilkenny met in October 1642 and adopted the motto "Pro Deo, Pro Rege, Pro

Partia Hibernia Unanimio," in effect declaring itself firmly behind the king. For the next several years, until the arrival of Cromwell in August 1649, Ireland was dominated by the "war of the three kingdoms."

The king ordered his Irish representatives, Ormonde and Clanricarde, to enter into negotiations with the Catholic Confederacy. When a truce was arranged between Ormonde and the confederacy in September 1643, Munro, who had come as the king's representative, would not accept it. He subsequently signed the Solemn League and Covenant with his fellow Scots and the English parliamentarians. Those who signed the Solemn League and Covenant pledged themselves to "extirpate Papacy and Prelacy, to preserve the liberties of the kingdom and to lead holy lives themselves."[14] In Ulster the work of administering the oath was put under the charge of Rev. James Hamilton. He brought over Scottish ministers to serve as commissioners in 1644. Accompanied by an escort of calvary to protect them from roaming bands of enemy soldiers, they toured the provinces. Wherever the commissioners stopped, they explained the covenant's provisions to the local citizens and secured many signatures. An estimated sixteen thousand people, including many in Munro's army, were reported to have signed the covenant.

While the covenant was being signed, Munro's operations in Ulster were being hampered by a lack of money, arms, ammunition, food, and clothes, which his newfound allies, the English parlimentarians, had promised to supply. The money, which had been originally raised by the English Parliament for the war in Ireland, was now used to wage the war against King Charles. The winter of 1645 was a cold, hard one for Munro's Scottish regiments, and they were forced to live off the country. Conditions worsened to the point that, in 1644, many of Munro's troops began to return home, against orders. The Ulster Scots became alarmed at the prospect of being left unprotected but the situation improved when supplies began to arrive in April 1644.

The Catholic Confederacy was having its problems too. It was split between the Old English, who were predominantly loyal to the king and wanted a quick end to the war, and the native Irish, who were mainly concerned with recovering their confiscated land and were willing to fight the war to the bitter end to achieve their objective. The disunity and rivalry in the confederate ranks can be seen in the fact that the confederacy could not appoint a single commander-in-chief. Owen Roe O'Neill, the nephew of the great earl of Tyrone, commanded the forces in Ulster, while Thomas Preston had command in Leinster. Both had distinguished themselves in the Spanish Netherlands. There a jealous rivalry had developed, making cooperation in Ireland impossible.

Despite this serious problem, O'Neill managed to inflict a crushing defeat on Munro at Benburb on June 5, 1646. The Scottish army was routed; its losses amounted to 3,000 men, compared to only 70 for the Irish. In addition, 1,500 horses and two months' worth of provisions for the Scottish army were captured. Throughout Ulster, panic gripped the Scottish Presbyterians, and many fled once again to Scotland. O'Neill, however, failed to follow up and instead stopped to relish his smashing victory. Had he marched on to Carrickfergus, O'Neill probably would have conquered Ulster and changed the course of the war in Ireland.

The Irish political situation now grew more complex as a number of factions fought to achieve their own ends, making any kind of an alliance impossible. Everything was in an extreme state of confusion when Cromwell came to Ireland in 1649 with fifteen thousand troops. The civil war in England had been won and Charles I executed. Cromwell was sent to Ireland by the Council of State to crush the remaining royalist troops, who were now in alliance with the Irish Catholic rebels. Cromwell was a shrewd politician and brilliant soldier to whom the disorganized native Irish had no answer.

Fired by a desire to avenge the atrocities committed in Ulster during the uprising in 1641, Cromwell embarked on a ruthless campaign to bring Ireland under his control. He justified his actions by saying, "I am persuaded that this is a righteous judgment of God upon the barbarous wretches, who have imbued their hands with much innocent blood."[15] Even to this day, the Catholic Irish equate Cromwell's name with cruelty. For many years, the worst possible condemnation from an Irishman were the words "the curse of Cromwell be upon you."[16] Stories are still told of a compact that Cromwell supposedly made with the devil.

Cromwell began his Irish campaign at Drogheda in September 1649. The defense of the city was stubborn, and in anger, Cromwell forbade his troops "to spare any that were in arms in the town." As a result, unarmed women and even priests were slaughtered. Cromwell wrote home of the massacre: "It hath pleased God to bless our endeavors at Drogheda.... The enemy was about 3,000 in the town.... I do not think 30 of the whole number escaped with their lives. Those that did are safe in custody for the Barados.... I wish that all honest hearts may give the glory of this to God alone, to whom indeed the promise of this mercy belongs."[17]

From Drogheda, Cromwell marched through Ireland, crushing all opposition. At Wexford an even greater massacre occurred: 2,000 were killed, including 200 defenseless women and children who had sought refuge in a marketplace. Shortly afterward, with Ireland under control, Cromwell returned to England, leaving the mopping-up operations to his son-in-law Henry Ireton, who completed the task by 1652. Ireland, for the first time in its history, was completely subdued and lay at the mercy of the English.

The news of the beheading of Charles I in January 1649 had been received with revulsion by Presbyterians in Ireland and Scotland. The Presbytery of Belfast expressed its displeasure by boldly drafting a "representation" in February, which condemned the English Parliament and reaffirmed the Solemn League and Covenant. The great poet John Milton, who was also the mouthpiece of the English Parliament, wrote a reply, characterizing Belfast as a "barbarous nook" and accusing the Presbyterians of "as much devillish malice, impudence and false-hood as any Irish rebel could have uttered."[18]

Cromwell's Irish commissioners gave bite to Milton's remarks by drafting the Engagement Oath in 1650, making it compulsory and binding on those who had signed the covenant "to renounce the pretended title of Charles Stuart and the whole line of King James, and to be faithful to the Commonwealth."[19] Life again became difficult for those Scotch-Irish Presbyterians who refused to take the oath. Once more, many fled to Scotland.

When the military campaign ended in 1652, Puritan England went about the task of settling accounts with the Irish Catholic rebels. It decided that Ireland's capacity for rebellion must be broken once and for all. Most of the Irish rebels who surrendered were not killed but were sent into exile, either to Spain or to France. Some were sold into slavery in the West Indies. By the standards of the time, reprisals were minimal: only fifty-two people were executed, including one of the Irish leaders, Sir Phelim O'Neill.

It was necessary to compensate both the adventurers who had helped provide the financial means for Parliament to wage war and the army, which had fought months without pay. Originally, the plan had been to confiscate only 2.5 million acres of Irish land, but the war had dragged on and now, with more people to pay off, this was not enough. In 1652 the English Parliament passed an Act of Settlement. Out of the twenty million available acres, eleven million of the richest were confiscated to satisfy the claims of the creditors. The Irish were to be punished by their degree of involvement in the rebellion, although holders of less than ten pounds in property were given a pardon.

For the Irish Catholic landowners who couldn't prove their loyalty, the choice was "To Hell or Connaught."[20] This meant that land still held by the Roman Catholic landlords in Leinster, Munster, and Ulster had to be exchanged for some of the poorest, most infertile, and most barren land in Ireland. Even many of those who could prove that they had not taken part in the rebellion still lost what they had. The transplantation was confined to the landowners, their families, and retainers. The rest of the population—those who did not own land—stayed behind to serve their new Protestant settlers as "hewers of wood and drawers of water."

The impact of the war and the Cromwellian settlement that

followed was devastating. In the fighting that had lasted for more than a decade, an estimated half a million people—about 40 percent of the population—had from famine, war, and disease. The English policy of confiscation and resettlement drastically changed the balance of political power in Ireland. Before 1641, two-thirds of the land in Ireland was owned by the Catholic Irish. By 1660, more than two-thirds was in Protestant possession.

Cromwell's severe policies were also applied to the Scotch-Irish Presbyterians, particularly those in Antrim and Down, who were now regarded as being as untrustworthy as the Catholic Irish. Cromwell decided that the Presbyterians should be transplanted away from the Scottish mainland. According to a government plan, approximately 260 people were to remove themselves from Ulster to Tipperary, Kilkenny, and Waterword by May 1654, on penalty of death; however, permission to delay their departure was freely given. When Cromwell's son Henry became lord deputy of Ireland, the situation relaxed, and the transportation south was not carried out.

Despite its tenuous position, the Scottish colony in northern Ireland continued to grow during the nine years of Cromwell's rule. The wars of the 1640s had strengthened the bond between the Ulster community and Scotland. Despite the bloodshed and devastation, the colony's population had managed to increase, mainly because of a steady immigration from Scotland, which continued through the rest of the century. In 1654 Henry Cromwell officially ended the persecution against the Presbyterian Church when he granted each Presbyterian minister who applied a stipend of £100 a year. Five years later forty-nine Presbyterian ministers were receiving grants. Many Presbyterian ministers were permitted to preach under the ecclesiastical control of the state church.

In 1653 there were only six Presbyterian ministers in all of Ulster. By 1660 there were seventy, who had charge of 100,000 worshippers in eighty parishes. The overwhelming majority of the Presbyterians were Scots. An Irish *State Paper* of 1660 stated, "There are 40,000 Irish and 80,000 Scots in Ulster, ready to bear arms and not above 5,000 English in the whole province beside the army."[21]

When Oliver Cromwell died in 1658, his eldest son, Richard, assumed the leadership; however, he soon proved to be incompetent. So, ironically, just eleven years after the war, Cromwell's generals proclaimed Charles II king of England on May 14, 1660. Shortly before his restoration, Charles had issued the Declaration of Breda, which encouraged all to believe that his reign would be one of religious toleration. Many Presbyterians were foolish enough to suppose that the Solemn League and Covenant, which Charles II had been forced to swear to in 1650, would be honored. Charles' first act was to restore the Episcopalian Church to its preeminent position in England, Scotland, and Ireland. In 1661 the Act of Uniformity was passed, which declared that "incumbents were to use the book of Common Prayer under pain of deprivation."[22] Anyone administering the sacrament without being Episcopally ordained was liable to a fine of £500. The House of Lords further declared that "anyone who by word or deed defended the Covenant should be deemed an enemy to his sacred majesty, the public peace and the church."[23]

In the British Isles and Ireland, over two thousand Presbyterian and Puritan ministers were ejected from the pulpit. Of the sixty-eight Presbyterians in the north of Ireland, only seven obeyed the decrees. The rest were forbidden to preach or to perform marriages, baptisms, or any other duty of ministry without first confirming and being Episcopally ordained. Jeremy Taylor, whose diocese of Conor, Down, and Dromore was in the main area of Presbyterian power, decreed thirty-six parishes vacant in one day. Bishop Leslie of Raphoe first excommunicated and then imprisoned four Presbyterian ministers and held them in jail for six years. Many congregations were forced to go without a minister; others, despite the danger and the fear of imprisonment, met secretly at night to hear their ministers preach.

After an attempted coup in 1663, persecution became very intense. Although the "Blood's Plot" involved men in the south of

Ireland who had Cromwell party sympathies and included only one Presbyterian named William Lecky, the government ordered all Presbyterian ministers to be thrown in jail. Some managed to flee to Scotland, but many others languished in prison until the lord lieutenant became convinced of their innocence. After a few years, matters returned to normal, and ministers slowly began to return to their Irish congregations.

The first sign of relief for the Scotch-Irish from persecution in Ireland during the reign of Charles II came in 1672 when he started the practice of giving a state grant to the Presbyterian ministers. This grant, which became known as the Regium Donum, or King's Gift, at first amounted to £600 a year and marked the beginning of state support for the Irish Presbyterian Church. The gift continued, with a slight interval, until the passage of the Disestablishment Act of 1869. Although by this action the Presbyterian Church in Ireland was officially recognized, the threat of persecution remained in effect throughout King Charles' reign. In 1664, for example, the Antrim and Down meetinghouses were closed by force and public worship by Presbyterians was prohibited.

Despite the oppression, the Scottish colony remained strong and continued to increase steadily in size. In his survey of Ireland in 1672, Sir William Petty concluded that there were 100,000 Scots, compared with 800,000 Irish and 200,000 English. The growth of the colony was helped by events in Scotland, where Charles' repressive measures had fomented rebellion on the part of the stubborn Covenanters of the western lowlands, who refused to accept Episcopacy. In 1670 the Scottish government passed the notorious "Black Act," which made field preaching punishable by death. Harassed when they tried to hold their meetings in secret, the Covenanters armed themselves. Fighting broke out; many were killed, hanged, or tortured, while others were thrown in prison. Later, some were sold into slavery in the colonies. In 1679 a poorly led army of Covenanters was decisively defeated in a pitched battle at Bothwell Bridge.

The persecution that followed was merciless. The Test Act,

passed in 1681, compelled the rebels to accept the complete authority of the king in all church and civil matters and to renounce their Presbyterianism. Courts were set up to strictly enforce the act. This was too much for the Covenanters. The religious situation in the north of Ireland seemed good compared with their treatment, and so thousands of Scots migrated in the early 1680s. Shortly thereafter, however, events in Ireland would stop this migration, and once more Scots would return to the British Isles.

4

The Siege of Derry and the Protestant Triumph

The fortunes of the Scotch-Irish began to change in 1685 when Charles II suffered a stroke and died at the age of fifty-five. A priest was smuggled up the back stairs to enable the king to die in peace as a Catholic. Actually, Charles' death brought a change in the fortunes of all Irish Protestants because to the throne came Charles' ardently Catholic brother James II, who immediately began to adopt measures that would restore the full scope of royal power and the supremacy of the Catholic religion in England and Ireland.

Uneasy about the new monarch, the Irish Protestants became worried by the quick dismissal of the lord lieutenant, the duke of Ormonde, whose Protestant sympathies were not in accord with James' plans for Ireland. James the dispatched Richard Talbot, now the earl of Tyrconnel, to Ireland to carry out his policies. Talbot was an arch anti-Protestant with a political outlook colored by the events of his early life. As a child, he had survived the destruction of Drogheda and had witnessed the slaughter of three thousand men, women, and children. This experience had hardened Talbot, making him the perfect instrument for James' Catholic program.

Talbot's appointment uplifted the spirits of the Irish Roman Catholics and brought them hope that their deliverance from the yoke of English tyranny had finally arrived. As Catholics, they hoped that James would give them preferential treatment in order to help them survive amid a growing Protestant population that had recently swelled as a result of an influx of Protestant refugees. The Huguenots were the largest group of immigrants. In 1685, France had revoked the Edict of Nantes, which had guaranteed them religious liberty. An estimated half million fled the country, many of whom came to the north of Ireland. Being staunch Calvinists, most of the Huguenots settled in Scotch-Irish communities and joined the Presbyterian Church. They were an industrious people whose skills helped improve the methods of manufacturing linen, which eventually became a vital part of the Ulster economy.

The Catholics were encouraged when Talbot began publicly to attack the Act of Settlement and talked about giving the land back to the dispossessed native Irish. Appointed commander-in-chief of the Irish army, Talbot began to pursue James' policies earnestly by making the army predominantly Catholic. Between 200 and 300 Protestant officers were purged. Those who had paid for their commissions were not automatically compensated but had to go to Dublin at their own expense to press their claims. In addition, 6,000 to 8,000 soldiers were discharged. By the end of 1687, Talbot had completely reorganized the army.

He next turned his attention to the civil administration, replacing the Protestant revenue officers, sheriffs, and justices of the peace and reinstating Catholics at the bar, in the privy council, and as aldermen. Civic charters were recalled and predominantly Catholic corporations appointed. By 1688 Catholics had placed Protestants from most of the chief administrative posts.

During the fall of 1688, Irish Protestants became increasingly alarmed at the state of affairs. The pace of the exodus, which began in the summer, quickened as many sold their possessions, closed down their houses, and moved to England and Scotland. Those who stayed lived in fear; many believed that a repetition of the events of 1641 was imminent. Rumors abounded in all parts of Ireland, heightening the growing sense of uneasiness and the anxiety of the Protestants. There was talk that blacksmiths were making arms for the use of the Catholic population and that priests at mass were "telling of the great plans that were afoot which would affect the whole nation."[1] The circulation of a number of anonymous letters fueled suspicions. One such letter was found on the streets of Cumber, County Down, on December 3, 1688. The letter, professed to be written by a friend, was addressed to Lord Mount-Alexander, a Protestant nobleman who lived in the town. It read:

> Good my Lord,
>   I have written to let you know that all our Irishmen through Ireland is sworn: that on the nineth day of this month they are all to kill and murder man, wife, and child; and I desire your lordship to take care of yourself, and all others that are judged by our men to be heads, for whosoever of them can kill any of yours, they are to have a captain's place; so my desire to your honour is, to look to yourself, and give other noblemen warning and go not out either night or day without a good guard for you, and let no Irishman come near you, whatsoever he be; so this is all from him who was your father's friend, and is your friend, and will be, though I dare not be known, as yet, for fear of my life.[2]

Today, this letter is generally regarded as a hoax, but at the time, the Protestants took it very seriously, and copies were distributed all over Ireland, causing a general panic. On December 7, a copy reached the city of Derry. At about the same time, news arrived that a garrison of Catholic troops under the command of the earl of Antrim was being sent to the city to relieve Lord Mountjoy's regiment, one of the few essentially Protestant units left in Ireland. Mountjoy's regiment was supposed to have been replaced no later than November 23, but the move was delayed two weeks to give Antrim time to organize his regiment. Determined to command a fine-looking body of tall men, the eccentric earl spent some time searching for recruits who were at least six feet tall. Enlistment was slow too because many of the Irish believed that Antrim's regiment was ultimately destined for service in England, and they did not want any part of this. When Antrim's regiment failed to reach Derry on the appointed date, Mountjoy, in accordance with his orders, left the city and marched south. Derry was temporarily left without a garrison.

The two weeks before the eventual arrival of Antrim proved to be a critical point in Irish history. It gave the citizens of Derry time to think and talk among themselves and finally convince many people that the coming of Antrim was part of an overall plan to kill Protestants. However, despite the myth of Protestant unity in the face of the enemy, not all the city was willing to defy royal authority. When there was talk of closing the gates and keeping Antrim's troops out, many of the older people were hesitant because to do so would be tantamount to an act of treason, since James was still the legitimate king. The younger element, however, was less cautious. With all the rumors of a possible massacre circulating, they thought it foolish to allow the royal garrison to enter. They wanted to close the gates and take their chances.

The debate was continuing in earnest on December 7 when lookouts on the city's walls spotted Antrim's troops at the waterside, making their way in boats across the Foyle River. Two of Antrim's regiments were admitted to the city. They presented their papers and demanded lodging for their men and forage for their horses. While the city's officials considered allowing the regiment in, thirteen apprentice boys seized the initiative, drew their swords, and slammed the gates in the astonished faces of Antrim's troops, who stood just sixty yards away. Threatened with gunfire, Antrim withdrew to the other side of the river.

The memory of the actions of the thirteen apprentices is perpetuated today in the brotherhood of the Apprentice Boys of Derry, which has seven parent clubs in Derry and branches throughout Ulster and in England, Scotland, and America. In Derry stands the Apprentice Boys Hall, built in 1873. Each December 7 the Protestants of Derry, wearing the sashes of the Orange Order and other ceremonial garb, assemble to celebrate the actions of the apprentice boys who helped the Protestant cause and were instrumental in saving Ireland for William of Orange.

Meanwhile, not sure that he was strong enough to take the city and not wanting to engage in a skirmish without the approval of higher authorities, the earl of Antrim decided to retreat as far as the city of Antrim. The citizens of Derry realized how ill-prepared they were to face the enemy, and they sent an emissary to London to ask for help. To make the city safe, all Catholics were removed outside of the walls.

Aware of their vulnerability, the Protestants in the Ulster countryside fled for the safety of the chief strongholds of Derry and Enniskillen. In doing so, they adopted a "scorched earth" policy, burning their homes and destroying their crops. One French officer, who later came to Ireland with James, noted that "only three miserable cabins stood in a stretch of forty miles. Everything else was rock, bog, and moor."[3] All of Antrim and Lisburn—thirty thousand Protestants of both sexes and all ages—poured into Derry. Others sought the safety of another stronghold, Enniskillen. In describing the exodus to the cities, the English historian MacAulay wrote:

> The flight seems wild and tumultuous. The fugitives broke down the bridges and burned the ferry boats. Whole towns, the seats of the Protestant population, were left in ruins without one inhabitant. The people of Cavan migrated in one body to Enniskillen. The day was wet and stormy. The road was deep in mire. It was a piteous sight to see, mingled with the men, the women and children weeping, famishing and tolling through the mud up to their knees.[4]

When the news of Derry's defiance reached Dublin, the earl of Tyrconnel was so angry that he burned his wig by throwing it in the fire, a gesture he usually made when upset by bad news. Only three days before, Mountjoy had arrived in Dublin after a tiring march from the north. Immediately, Talbot ordered Mountjoy back, with six companies of his regiment, to reoccupy the city. Ulster

Protestants greatly respected Mountjoy; thus, when he reached Derry, the city's citizens appointed a committee to meet with him. Mountjoy offered them generous terms: a general pardon, the right to retain their arms, and a guarantee of safe conduct from the city for any families who wanted to leave. In late December 1688, an agreement was reached whereby only two companies, both Protestant and commanded by Robert Lundy, were admitted to the city.

While Catholic power had increased in Ireland, loyalty to James had ebbed in England. On November 5, 1688, William of Orange landed with his army of fifteen thousand at Turbay in England. William traveled through the country, gaining adherents. Meanwhile support, for James withered away, forcing him to flee to France. The vacant throne was offered to William and his wife, Mary, as joint sovereigns, and they were crowned on April 11, 1689.

In southern Ireland, Talbot received word of William's succession and began to prepare for war. Over Dublin Castle flew a flag defiantly carrying the slogan "Now or Never, Now or Forever!" Irish Catholic peasants left their fields and flocked to Dublin to join the army. They were fired by their hatred of the English and the belief that the injustices of the past several decades were to be finally righted. Priests added to the excitement by urging their congregations to take up arms and prepare for the day of liberation. The Irish army, which had consisted of only eight regiments, now swelled to forty-eight. By February 1689 an estimated 100,000 Irishmen were armed, of whom 50,000 were soldiers.

While the Catholics readied themselves for war, the citizens of Derry prepared for the city's defense. Food was stored away; the gates were locked; and no one was allowed to enter the city without official permission. One merchant was sent to Scotland to buy arms and supplies with money contributed by some of Derry's wealthier citizens, but Scottish aid turned out to be meager. The merchant managed to bring back only forty-two barrels of gunpowder, ten of which he left in County Down for the defense of the area. David Cairnes, the emissary who had been sent to seek help from King William, reached London near the end of January.

William agreed that military supplies should be sent at once to Derry. To boost the city's morale, he gave Cairnes a letter to take back to Derry. It informed city officials of the "King's concern for the city, evidenced by the arms and ammunition he had already sent, and the further preparations he was making not only for the defence of Londonderry but also for the recovery of the whole kingdom."[5]

In the middle of February, James, with the blessing of Louis XIV, left France for Ireland. Louis believed that the time was ripe to weaken England's position on the continent by an attack at its back door. In September 1688, Louis had launched his armies into Rhineland, hoping to increase his influence and disrupt his enemies. William of Orange had taken the lead against Louis with the resources of England behind him and the active help of the emperor, Spain, and Brandenburg and the tacit support of the pope. Louis, however, now was reluctant to chance a large army on James, the monarch who had given up his kingdom to William and Mary without a fight. Instead, the French king gave James about four hundred officers, in the hope that they could perform the difficult task of reorganizing and disciplining the Irish army and leading it to victory. The expedition also carried about fifty thousand gold crowns, today's equivalent of a little over one million dollars.

When the ships docked at Kinsdale, County Cork, on March 12, the Irish Catholics in the area gave James a joyous welcome. Two days later James met with Talbot and his military advisors, who reported that all was going well in the field. The Protestants in the three southern provinces of Munster, Leinster, and Connaught had been completely subdued and disarmed, while in Ulster only Derry and Enniskillen, among the towns of any importance, acknowledged William. Talbot expressed no doubts that the resistance of these two towns would soon be crushed. On March 24 James triumphantly arrived in Dublin, the first English monarch to visit the Irish capital since Richard II three hundred years earlier. He immediately exerted his authority by issuing a series of proclamations, which included a command to all Protestants who had recently left the kingdom to return and accept the royal protection or face stiff penalties for refusal.

While James was defining his position in Dublin, Talbot was busy striking the first blows against the Protestant insurgents in the north. His prime objective was to break the resistance before help arrived from England. To accomplish the task, he sent Lieutenant General Richard Hamilton north with twenty-five hundred troops. As Hamilton advanced, the Protestant forces retreated in the direction of Derry, where citizens met in a council of war and decided to send troops to engage the Catholic army before it reached the city.

When the two armies met on April 15, Hamilton's troops, although outnumbered five to one, proved victorious. Colonel Robert Lundy, the commander-in-chief of the Protestant army, already looked on with suspicion by many of Derry's citizens, was accused of treachery. Accounts indicate that Lundy was one of the first to flee the battle. When the retreating army arrived back in Derry, they found the gates closed and Lundy safely inside. Eight thousand troops had to spend the night outside the gates at the mercy of the Irish Catholic army.

On the same day as the battle, two ships carrying two regiments of Williamites, plus a supply of arms and ammunition, anchored in Lough Foyle. The next day the commander, Colonel John Cunningham, went to Derry and met with Lundy and a number of his officers. Cunningham gave Lundy William's letter of instructions, which expressed the hope "that things shall be in such a posture, as that we may, with the blessing of God, restore in a short time our kingdom of Ireland to its former peace and tranquility."[6]

The council of war was packed with Lundy's men, who decided that the situation was hopeless. A resolution was passed stating that the town could not be defended. Although it was agreed that the decision would not be revealed to the people, word leaked out. Many hardliners in the city were outraged. Lundy, placed virtually under house arrest, sent a message to Cunningham, begging the colonel not to leave without him "lest he become a sacrifice to the reliable."[7] But soon after, the ships returned to England. Eventually Lundy did manage to escape from Ireland—as a common soldier carrying a load of matchwood on his back. Lundy's actions at Derry have earned him, among the Protestants of Northern Ireland today, a reputation akin to that of Benedict Arnold in the United States. Today the name "Lundy" is used as a derogatory term for any Protestant who weakens in his zealous fervor for the Protestant cause.

At this point it seemed to James that the conquest of Derry and Enniskillen was imminent. Against the advice of Talbot, he decided to march north and join his army. Leaving Dublin on April 15, the king and his royal entourage experienced a miserable journey. The fleeing Protestants and the advancing Irish armies had laid waste to the land. A French officer who accompanied James compared the journey to "travelling through the deserts of Arabia." In reference to James' troops he said, "No matter their class, they all ate what they could and drank water, or detestable beer, made with oats instead of barley, and flavored with some merciless herb as a substitute for hops."[8]

Reaching Derry, James confidently expected that the city's citizens would give him a royal welcome when they learned of his approach to the city. A messenger sent by James was told that Derry's residents would give their answer in an hour's time. The answer came in the form of a fusillade of musket and cannon shot, which killed some of James' troops.

Despite the gunfire, the city appeared indecisive about whether to resist or to surrender. According to some accounts, several citizens met with James and assured him that it was only some of the "drunken rabble" who had seized the guns and fired, without the approval of the city's authorities. Believing that Derry could not hold out for long, James offered its citizens "their lives, estates, freedom of religion and a pardon for all their past offenses."[9] The offer, however, was refused. James himself now appeared before Derry's walls in the belief that his mere appearance would cause the city to capitulate. Advancing toward Derry, he was shocked to be greeted by gunfire and to see some of his own personal bodyguard fall dead beside him. As he scurried for safety, James could hear the cries of "No Surrender!" from the defiant Protestants.

James continued to send letters in the hope that he could persuade the city to capitulate. After receiving a second letter, Derry's citizens decided to hold a meeting to consider the king's latest offer. After some discussion, the city's moderates agreed to send twenty men to James to negotiate. But when these men tried to leave, they were prevented by the more hardline element in the city. Instead, James was sent a reply that read, "The course we have undertaken, we design forever to maintain; and question not, but that powerful providence which has hitherto been our Guardian, will finish the protection of us against all your attempts, and give a happy issue to one army."[10]

James still refused to give up, and he sent a carte blanche signed by himself, asking the city to write in their own terms of surrender. Receiving no reply, a frustrated James returned to Dublin, leaving Maumont in command.

So began what has been known in Irish history as the "Siege of Derry." It was a strange sort of siege, though; in fact, if we look at the size of the two opposing forces and the firepower they had available, it is difficult to call what occurred at Derry a *siege* in any usual meaning of the term. The Jacobite troops outside the walls were too small to successfully besiege the city. Their numbers totaled a mere 6,000, while inside the city was a larger force of 7,000 men. As the historian Tony Gray has pointed out, "Napoleon had said that to be successful a besieged city should be at least four times the strength of the garrison it is attending."[11] In addition, the Jacobite troops lacked the necessary artillery to shell the city into submission. When the siege began, they had only three field pieces, two siege guns, and two small mortars whereas the city had thirty pieces of artillery in all.

One of James' officers complained that out of every ten muskets, only one might be counted on to fire properly. The besieging force not only was ill-armed and ill-equipped but also lacked the military training to carry out its objective. James' troops were led by a number of inexperienced officers, composed mainly of "trailors, butlers and shoemakers," as one of the French officers in James' entourage put it. Many of the Jacobite soldiers were undisciplined, raw recruits who had to face their adversary from pitched tents out in the open in the face of terrible Irish weather, without proper medical attention and supplies.

Over the years, as the events at Derry became indelibly a part of the folk memory for Northern Ireland Protestants, many myths have evolved about the "siege." For example, in a true siege, the city would be closed. Yet throughout the spring and summer of 1689, a steady stream of refugees poured into Derry, and Protestant troops from the surrounding countryside continued to enter the city and reinforce the garrison.

Another myth has been the idea that the city posed a united front to the enemy. As we have seen earlier and as was to be the case right up to the relief of Derry, many within the city's gates wanted to surrender. The enemy even had constant knowledge of what was happening inside the gates. As would not be the case in true siege, the Derry garrison was always ready to venture out and do battle, often inflicting heavy casualties on the enemy. In one skirmish, a principal officer of the Jacobite forces was killed. A great mystery of the siege—and there have been many—is why the Protestants, who were better armed and equipped than the besieging power and situated in better living conditions, did not act more aggressively and go out more often to do battle with the enemy.

Despite all this, the siege began after James returned to Dublin. Both sides settled in for a protracted struggle. The Jacobite forces strengthened their position around Derry by taking the strategic fort of Culmore, which prevented supplies and men from reaching the city by sea, and Derg Castle (now known as Castle Derg), another strategic position on a narrow pass between Enniskillen and Derry.

The Jacobite military command discussed the best methods to

prevent ships from coming up the Foyle. The sinking of a couple of barges in the river was proposed. This idea was dismissed on the grounds that it would destroy the commerce of Derry and thereby reduce the royal revenue. Eventually the commanders decided to erect a barrier across the Foyle. A row of stakes were driven into the riverbed, and a series of large timber beams, tied tightly by ropes and chains and firmly fastened to the shore on each side by a cable, formed a barrier more than one-fourth of a mile in length. Forts and batteries lined each side of the Foyle.

Meanwhile, Derry's preparations for its defense continued. The city's inhabitants were organized into eight regiments under the command of appointed officers. Two of the regiments were ordered by the governor to remain on guard during the night. After eight in the evening, no drinking or lighting of candles was allowed. Ammunition was transferred from the main storage area to four other locations to prevent loss from fire and treachery. Considering the seriousness of the situation, the garrison received generous rations: each person was to have a salmon and a half, two pounds of salt beef, and four quarts of oatmeal a week.

For the most part, those massed inside Derry's gates tried to get along despite the crowded conditions. The Presbyterians formed the largest part of the city's population. Many were the forefathers of the Scotch-Irish who, a few generations later, would take part in the great migration to America. One of the most notable was James McGregor, who later helped fire a large gun from the cathedral tower announcing to the city that the relieving ships were on their way. In 1718 he immigrated to America and founded Londonderry, New Hampshire.

St. Columb's Cathedral became the spiritual center of the resistance. The vaults and lower parts of the church were used to store ammunition. The cathedral was used by both the Episcopalians and the Protestants for services. It was decided that the Episcopalians could have the cathedral on Sunday morning, and the Presbyterians would be allowed to use it on Sunday afternoon. But since the Presbyterians were so numerous, four to five other places of worship had to be found to accommodate all of the worshippers.

While both sides dug in for the siege of Derry, James assembled a parliament in Dublin, which met for ten weeks and became known as the Patriot Parliament. The parliament was entirely Roman Catholic, its aim being to destroy the Protestant power base. A series of laws stripped all Protestants—nobility, clergy, merchants, and yeomen—of their property and wealth, without compensation. But news of what was taking place in Dublin only strengthened the resolve of the people of Derry and Enniskillen. Protestant refugees, who were still fleeing to England, took reports of the measures being taken to suppress the Protestants. A concerned House of Commons appropriated 11,000 for the relief of the refugees, and a committee was appointed to investigate what measures were being taken to help the beleaguered Protestants in northern Ireland.

The months of May and June were marked by minor skirmishes, with casualties relatively light and with little accomplished on either side. By early June the Jacobite forces intensified their bombardment of Derry. Between June 3 and June 8, nearly 160 small bombs were hurled into the city. In some instances, the roofs and tops of houses came crashing down, crushing many people to death. A number of the dead were sick people who were unable to leave their houses.

During this bombardment, a relieving force of thirty ships arrived from England. Spotting the ships, the city rejoiced. Hope seemed to have arrived at last. Signs were flashed from both the ships and the city in an effort to make contact. All was in vain, however since no prearranged code had been determined. A boat was sent from Derry, but it turned back after heavy fire. Of the two attempts made to send couriers from the ships through enemy lines, one did manage to make it through. The courier tried to send information back to the fleet from the cathedral's steeple but was unsuccessful. After much discussion aboard ship, it was decided that the boom could not be broken and that it would be unwise to try and relieve Derry. The ships withdrew to the middle of the lough, where they remained inactive for several weeks.

With a little more determination, the Protestants of Derry might have broken the siege at this point. The Irish army showed that it had no real taste for the fighting. At the first sight of the ships, the Jacobite forces took down their tents, removed their guns and bombs, evacuated their sick and wounded, and prepared to abandon the siege. But when nothing happened, they returned and resumed their positions.

The joy that the city had felt at the sight of the ships turned to despair—a despair made worse by deteriorating conditions. The large number of people in the city—by now estimated to be between twenty and thirty thousand—had almost exhausted the food, and water was in short supply. The garrison was reduced to eating horse meat. Despite the dangerous situation, people ventured outside the gate in search of weeds and herbs. The authorities began to conduct house-to-house searches to ensure that no one hoarded any food. The unsanitary conditions led to an outbreak of disease, which took countless lives. It was reported that in one day alone, fifteen officers died of fever.

In Dublin, James was becoming increasingly concerned that no progress was being made toward ending the siege. He sent his commander-in-chief, General Conrad de Rosen, north to expedite the situation. Rosen arrived at the Irish camp on June 17. After the city rejected his initial peace offer, Rosen decided to adopt tougher measures. On June 30 he sent the city an order: if the town had not surrendered by 6 P.M. on July 1, all the Protestants in the neighboring area would be gathered up and herded under Derry's walls. The city would either have to admit them (a ploy to further reduce Derry's dwindling supplies) or watch them starve or be slaughtered in the crossfire. The order added that when the city was finally captured, no mercy would be shown to its inhabitants.

When the city ignored the threat, Rosen proceeded to put his plan into operation. On July 2, the first group of about two hundred Protestants were marshaled toward Derry's walls. The city mistook them for the enemy and fired on them. Realizing who they were, the city stopped the firing before anyone got hurt. Thousands of Protestants were then herded, like animals, into roofless enclosures, which had previously been used for quartering cattle outside the walls. The cries of the Protestant prisoners could be heard from inside the city. Rather than being weakened in its resolve, however, the city became more hardened and determined, realizing what it could expect if the fight was given up.

In retaliation, the city erected high gallows in full view of the enemy. A message was sent from the city: if the Protestants outside the city were not allowed to return to their homes, the city would begin hanging its Jacobite prisoners, one by one. James, receiving news of Rosen's actions, and became furious. He immediately sent orders to his commanding general to free the Protestants. Rosen, however, had already concluded that his plan could not succeed. The prisoners were released from their cages and given provisions for their journey home.

Rosen's actions served only to toughen Derry's resistance. Its leadership now became almost fanatical in its determination to outlast the besieging force. The Reverend George Walker wrote that although the city's residents were forced to live on mice, rats, dogs, horse flesh, and whatever else could be found, they "unanimously resolved to eat the Irish and then one another, rather than surrender to anyone but their own King William and Queen Mary."[12]

Negotiations were resumed again in mid-July. Although lengthy discussions were held, the differences could not be worked out, and the talks came to an end. By this time, the situation within Derry had gone from bad to worse and was deteriorating by the hour. According to one eyewitness account, people were dying so quickly that room could scarcely be found to inter them. Even backyards and gardens were filled with graves, and some corpses were thrown into cellars. In some instances, whole families were wiped out. Leprosy was now added to the diseases plaguing the garrison.

The shortage of food became so critical that on July 24 the

city sent out five hundred men to try to round up some cattle that were grazing nearby. James' troops were so surprised to see such a motley crew dare leave the city that they retreated in confusion. The incident became known as the "Battle of the Cows." The expeditionary force was successful in bringing back some supplies, ammunition, and food. Walker said of the city, "We were under so great necessity that we had nothing left unless we could prey upon one another."[13] Walker goes on to tell of one fat gentleman who, believing himself to be in great danger because of his weight, began to imagine that several of the garrison were looking on him with hungry eyes. The man thought it best that he hide himself for three days.

Even though the city's suffering increased day by day, the ships, anchored at the mouth of the Foyle, made no effort to bring relief; however, the determination of most of those within Derry's walls remained resolute. John Hunter, a soldier who was in Derry throughout the siege, described how he could barely speak or walk. "Yet when the enemy was coming ... I found my former strength return to me ... there were many of us that could hardly stand on our feet before the enemy attacked the walls, who when they were attacking the out-trenches, ran against them more nimbly and with great courage."[14]

Around the middle of July, a message got through to the ships that Derry could not hold out much longer. Three ships—the *Swallow*, the *Phoenix*, and the *Jerusalem*—were stocked with provisions and set sail up the Foyle, eventually anchored near Culmore. There they waited for a favorable wind that would give them an opportunity to break the boom. The night of July 25 was chosen as D day.

It was Sunday evening and Reverend Walker had just delivered a sermon, asking the Lord to deliver the city from its enemies. About an hour after the sermon ended, sentinels on the city walls spotted the relief ships sailing up the Lough. Those who were strong enough made their way to the walls to see if, at last, the ships were actually coming to their rescue.

One ship struck the boom, recoiled, and ran aground in the shallow water on the right bank of the river. As the citizens of Derry watched, their hopes soared or subsided with each further attempt at the boom. Making matters more difficult for the relieving party was the heavy fire from the Jacobite shore artillery. It was the *Phoenix* that finally managed to slip through a break in the boom and gain the honor of being the first to arrive at Derry's quay. The whole episode took three hours. The relief, which the garrison had been expecting for three months, had finally come. After 105 days, the Siege of Derry was over.

Most of the garrison mustered the strength to welcome their rescuers. Supplies were unloaded and rations immediately distributed. Relief had arrived in the nick of time. According to Reverend Walker, the city had two days' worth of supplies left, which amounted to nine lean horses and a pint of meal per person.

It is estimated that out of Derry's fighting force of 7,000, which had begun the siege, only 3,000 survived. About 10,000 out of the 20,000 to 30,000 people who had crowded into the city perished. In eighty-nine days, 587 bombs had been hurled into the city. The entire population had become a horde of diseased, hollow-eyed, starving skeletons, kept alive only by the intensity of their faith and their determination to save the city from the Catholic enemy. James' troops continued to shell the city throughout the night and the following three days. Finally, they accepted defeat and withdrew, devastating the countryside as they marched back to the south.

The citizens of Derry were delighted to learn that their fellow Protestants who had found refuge in Enniskillen had also been successful against the enemy. When the Jacobites had prepared for an attack, Enniskillen had boldly sent out a force of about 2,500 to wage battle. Although outnumbered two-to-one and facing a better-equipped force, the Protestants scored a decisive victory at Newtonbutler, killing 2,500 of the Irish and taking another 500 prisoner. In comparison, Enniskillen's casualties were light: 20 killed and 50 wounded.

The valor of Derry's and Enniskillen's citizens proved decisive in the struggle between William of Orange and James II. Although firmly established in Munster, Connacht, and Leinster, James had failed miserably in Ulster. Wasting time and energy in a stubborn siege of the two Protestant strongholds in the north, James threw away his chance to invade first Scotland and then England. James did have strong support in Scotland, and if the two cities of Ulster had not held out as they did, he might have had a good chance to regain his throne. Instead, William was given time to raise a large army in England and build a bridgehead to Ireland.

In August 1689, 10,000 of William's troops, under the command of seventy-five-year-old Marshall Shomberg, were allowed to land unopposed in Ireland at Groomspart, County Down. The composition of the invading army showed the international character of the war that was now engulfing the European continent. The force included not only British soldiers but also Danish mercenaries, French Huguenots, and Netherlanders, all opposed to Louis XIV and France. They quickly occupied Belfast and Carrickfergus, but when James advanced to Drogheda with 20,000 men, Shomberg decided that his army was too small to engage the enemy. Instead, he set up quarters for the winter.

On June 14, 1690, King William himself landed at Carrickfergus with an army of 36,000. As he marched south to engage his archenemy James, bonfires were lit on all the hills of Antrim and Down. A deputation from the Presbyterian Church in Belfast greeted the king and expressed its loyalty. In gratitude, William ordered the collector of customs at Belfast to authorize the payment of £1,200 a year to the Presbyterian ministers of Ulster.

On July 12 the most famous battle in Irish history was fought at the Boyne River, which is located about thirty miles from Dublin. The battle was to have been fought the day before, but James had postponed it because of his superstitious anxiety about Mondays. It didn't matter, though, for James had little chance; his troops were outnumbered and ill-equipped. At the first possible moment, James showed his mettle by fleeing the battlefield. Although casualties were relatively light—1,500 on James' side and 400 on William's—

the battle took the lives of two Protestant heroes, Marshall Shomberg and Reverend Walker of Derry. Walker had returned to Ireland from a triumphant visit to London as one of the heroes of the Siege of Derry, where he had been received with a tremendous reception and had been given the bishopric of Derry. When King William heard of Walker's death at the Boyne, he supposedly exclaimed, "What the devil was he doing here?!"

The Battle of the Boyne marked the third time in a century that the Catholics had been defeated in a major battle. This time, however, the Protestant victory was decisive. It secured the permanent establishment of the Ulster colony and the political supremacy of the Protestants over the Catholics in Ireland. The twelfth of July, the anniversary of the battle, became an immortal day for the Irish Protestants, the occasion for an annual public holiday in Ulster. Each year several thousands of the Orange Order parade and march in honor of the "glorious and immortal" memory of William III. His face adorns the banners and appears on the street murals in Protestant neighborhoods.

When James fled the battlefield, he headed for Dublin and then on to France, never to return to Ireland. He made one more futile effort to persuade Louis to give him an army to try and regain his kingdom, but the French king refused, obviously not wanting to waste any more time, money, or arms. Meanwhile, James' Irish allies were left to fight against insurmountable odds, their hope being not victory but a better settlement. King William tried to break the Irish resistance by capturing Limerick, the main Irish stronghold, which was under the command of the brilliant Patrick Sarsfield. Failing in his objective, William returned to England, leaving his campaign to his subordinates.

After the Battle of the Boyne, the war dragged on for another fifteen months. When Limerick was besieged a second time, Sarsfield decided to sue for peace. In his desire to rid himself of the distracting Irish war, William offered generous terms of surrender, which were accepted. According to the Treaty of Limerick of October 2, 1691, those Catholic Irish soldiers who wanted to leave the country were guaranteed a pardon and safe passage to the Continent. Consequently, 11,000 sailed for France and joined the French army, in which they formed the famous Irish Brigade. This was the beginning of an exodus that became known as the "Flight of the Wild Geese." During the next century, thousands more Catholic soldiers left Ireland to become mercenaries all over the Continent, where they distinguished themselves in the European wars of the eighteenth and nineteenth centuries.

More important, the Protestant victory culminated in a series of acts that led to the further confiscation of Catholic-owned land, amounting to 1.5 million acres. It is estimated that the confiscation following the war reduced the area held by Catholic landowners to 500,000 "profitable" acres, or about one-fifteenth of the area of Ireland.

The civic articles of the Treaty of Limerick had promised the Roman Catholics the same degree of toleration that they had had under Charles II's reign. The treaty, however, required parliamentary confirmation, and the Dublin Parliament proved stubborn, refusing to ratify it. By the time the treaty was finally ratified in 1697, William had given way on many points, destroying the hope that the Catholics might once again participate in the life of the nation. Ironically, in the suppression that followed beginning in the early eighteenth century, not only Catholic but also Scotch-Irish Presbyterians would be affected.

5

Sailing West for the Promised Land

With King William now securely on the throne, it appeared that the long period of persecution endured by the Scotch-Irish was over. In a time of great danger to the British Crown, they had shown their mettle, proving to be staunchly loyal to the Protestant cause, and without their help and valor in the defense of Derry and Enniskillen, James would have been victorious and Ireland certainly would have once again come under Catholic influence. Furthermore, if the plantation was now firmly established in Ulster, it was the Scotch-Irish who undoubtedly deserved the credit; their industry and hard work had made it a success.

King William was quick to recognize the Scotch-Irish contribution, and in gratitude, he gave them more religious freedom than they had known in years. He also introduced measures making them legally more prosperous than they had been under James II. Encouraged by William's tolerance, many Scots who had fled Ireland because of Richard Talbot's repression began to return. Other Scots, meanwhile, eagerly flocked to Ireland to take advantage of the cheap land and the many opportunities that were now available. Between 1690 and 1697, an estimated fifty thousand Scots migrated across the North Channel, settling mainly in Ulster.

Soon, however, history began to repeat itself as the fortunes of the Scotch-Irish once again worsened. The death of King William in 1702 ushered in another period of persecution and insecurity.

With the succession of Queen Anne, the High Church party came to power in England, determined to enforce strict religious conformity. In 1704 the British Parliament passed the Test Act, which required "every person holding an office under the crown to take communion in the established church within three months of his appointment, failure to comply being regarded as the vacating of office."[1] Although aimed at Irish Catholics, the act actually affected all dissenting religious groups, including the Presbyterians. Like other dissenters, Presbyterians were excluded from the army, the military, the civil service, municipal corporations, and the teaching profession. At Belfast the entire city government was thrown out of office; Londonderry lost ten of its aldermen. According to the historian John Harrison, the Test Act "drove out of the corporation of Londonderry several of the very men who had fought through the siege of 1689."[2].

Most important, the Scotch-Irish Presbyterian ministers now had no official legal standing. Even marriages performed by them were considered null and void. "Many persons of undoubted reputation were prosecuted in the bishop's courts as fornicators for co-habitating with their wives, and their children were considered bastards," the historian James Leyburn has written.[3] The act allowed for fines to be levied on any Presbyterian minister who celebrated the Lord's Supper. In some parts of Ulster, the local authorities made up their own regulations, even going so far as not allowing dissenters to bury their dead unless an Episcopal minister officiated at the funeral and read the burial service of the Anglican Church.

Besides the Test Act, other forms of religious harassment occurred. When the English Parliament passed the Aburation Oath in 1703, for example, it became mandatory for all officeholders, including those in the church, to take an oath rejecting James II's claim to be king of England. Although professing their loyalty to the queen, four Presbyterian ministers of the Synod of Ulster refused, claiming that the oath implied the illegitimacy of James, which they considered to be untrue. Their refusal to take the oath led to legal action against them, and as other Scotch-Irish resisters had done in the seventeenth century, they fled Ireland. Throughout Queen Anne's reign, the English establishment made numerous efforts to curb the growth of the Presbyterian Church. Among other measures, it tried to suspend payment of the Regium Donum, a grant bestowed by Charles II to the Presbyterian clergy in Ulster in recognition of their loyalty. The chief exponent and architect of Anne's anti-Presbyterian policy was William King, bishop of Derry (1691–1703) and archbishop of Dublin (1703–30). Under King's leadership, the Episcopal Church got its wish, and the Regium Donum was withdrawn in 1704. But once again, the Scotch-Irish reacted in their typical stubborn manner, refusing to submit or to deny their faith. Despite the Crown's attempts at suppression, the Presbyterian Church continued to grow; by 1708 there were 130 congregations.

Besides religious persecution, the Scotch-Irish also experienced harsh economic discrimination. Beginning in the second half of the seventeenth century, the English government and the Irish landlords began to adopt measures and regulations that would ultimately lead to a mass exodus of thousands of Scotch-Irish across the Atlantic to seek a better life in the New World. The decline of the linen industry, repressive trade laws, and rack renting were the major economic factors.

The new restrictions on Irish trade were slow to come. In fact, for a very short period, Ireland had actually prospered. The Navigation Act of 1660 had placed Irish ships on an equal footing with those of England, allowing Ireland to trade directly with the colonies. Ireland thrived under the act; consequently, England began to look warily on Ireland as an economic rival. Gradually, the generous provisions of 1660 were withdrawn, and restrictions were placed on the trade between Ireland and the colonies.

The first major change in English policy occurred in 1663 with the passage of the Staple Act, which prevented all direct exports by Ireland to other colonies except for indentured servants and such vital necessities as horses and food. Another act, in 1671, further limited what Ireland could import from the colonies. Such restrictions, though exasperating, did not seriously jeopardize Ireland's welfare, since its chief product—foodstuffs—could still be exported. However, the woolen and linen industries in Ireland, particularly in the north, increased in prosperity in the closing years of the seventeenth century, arousing uneasiness among English competitors. In 1699 King William, under pressure from his country's business interests, forced the Irish Parliament to pass the Woolens Act, which prohibited the export of Irish wool to any place except England and Wales. This restriction left the foreign and colonial markets solely under control of the English, who could now set whatever price they wanted. This was a devastating blow to Ulster's most prosperous industry. As the historian R. J. Dickson points out, Ireland was "denied the privilege of intercolonial trading, a privilege denied to no other British colony."[4] These repressive laws were modified little during the course of the eighteenth century and remained in effect until after the outbreak of the American Revolution.

Only the manufacture of linen was tolerated. In the words of one English official, "It can be of no prejudice to Britain and is in a manner all that is left to Ireland and ought therefore to be encouraged as much as possible."[5] In the north especially, this led to an unhealthy dependence on linen manufacturing to supplement the meager profits of farming. It is estimated that throughout much of the eighteenth century, linen composed about half the total value of Ireland's exports.[6]

Although seemingly a cure for poverty, linen manufacturing actually brought hardship to the Scotch-Irish—a hardship on which the emigration trade was later to thrive. The hope of increased security provided by the extra income from linen was offset by the constantly increasing rent. In the words of one contemporary, "The price of land ... kept pace with the linen manufacture to the summit."[7] Also, those that relied solely on farming for a living were in direct competition for land with those that combined farming with linen manufacturing. The price of land rose constantly in the linen districts. Even if linen manufacturing became depressed for a while, the rent still went up, gobbling up any profits that were made from farming.

Later, in the latter part of the eighteenth century, the linen industry began to grow again, but ironically, even success spurred immigration. By 1775 flaxseed had become the principal import to northern Ireland, composing nearly three-fourths of its total from America. Boats came from Philadelphia and New York bringing hundreds of tons of flaxseed. Shipowners were eager for a paying cargo for the return voyage, and so linen goods were taken back to the colonies. Although flaxseed was bulky, linen did not take up much space, allowing plenty of room for people wanting to emigrate to America.

Besides sanctions, the Scotch-Irish faced another serious economic problem: the practice of rack-renting. Simply described, rack-renting was the landlord's habit of raising the rent when a lease on a tenant's land expired. With Ulster decimated by war, landlords during the 1690s were willing to rent land cheaply to tenants, especially to newcomers from Scotland. To further encourage emigration during this period, long leases were granted. The common term of lease in Ulster was for thirty-one years, a lot longer than in Scotland. The security of a long lease encouraged farmers to improve their land, extend their cultivation into wasteland, and practice enlightened farming methods.

After 1718, however, thousands of leases began to expire. Since land was now scarce, landowners could substantially raise their rents. Overnight, rents began to double and triple, and renters were forced to pay more than they could afford. The landlords did not really care about the fate of the tenants. In many cases, greed was their motivating factor, not the welfare of the local community.

Much of the Irish land was owned by absentee English landlords who rarely visited Ireland and had their revenue sent back to England. Many were extravagant spendthrifts who had large debts that had to be paid off. It was estimated that by 1729, £600,000 was being transferred abroad each year, a sum equaling about one-third of the total rents in Ireland. As Leyburn explains, "The landlord was unwilling to share the benefits with the farmers and only to raise their rents in moderate degrees, extracting from them all they possibly could, irrespective of their improvements, and what the tenant had done to make the property valuable."[8]

Protestant tenants who refused to pay the increased rents were evicted and replaced with poor Roman Catholics brought in from other areas, who were willing to accept a lower standard of living. Often, the landlord would put the land up for bid to get the highest possible rent. Angered by this practice, many Scotch-Irish refused to bid and lost their land. Others were outbid by Catholics, six or seven of whom would join together and pool their meager resources.

The land of opportunity now turned into a nightmare. "Within a single generation," says Leyburn, "the mood of the Protestant Ulster man had changed from optimism to gloom."[9] Edmund Kine, an estate manager in County Monaghan, described the depressing economic situation during the early 1720s:

> Money was never worse to get since I came here this
> 24 years than it is at this time for our market is all down.
> I knownot, the meaning of it, but it is believed here that it
> is occasioned by the hardship England is putting upon us ...
> the tenants have sold their grain and they can get no money
> when they have delivered it, but I hope the Spring will
> bring better markets or we will be broke altogether. We
> have had the saddest robbing in the country that ever was
> known and not only robbing but murdering, killing almost
> everywhere, where they rob. This is all occasioned by the
> scarceness of money.[10]

Thousands of Scotch-Irish, now dispossessed and without hope for the future, began to leave for the New World, the immigration bolstered by others who thought that if they stayed, they might lose everything too.

We have seen that an attempt by the Scotch-Irish to emigrate to America had come as early as 1636 when a group of brave Presbyterian clergymen and some of their parishioners tested the unknown but were forced back by the violent storms and rough seas of the Atlantic. No further effort was made until after 1780, when small numbers of Scotch-Irish began to leave Ulster for the American colonies, mainly because of religious persecution. This emigration came primarily from the Laggan and Foyle River valleys and was directed toward the area bordering the Chesapeake Bay. Among the emigrants was the Reverend Francis Makemie, who was later to earn the title of the "Father of American Presbyterianism." The missionary zeal of Makemie, a Scotch-Irishman from County Donegal, helped organize the first Presbyterian Church in the colonies.

The first substantial Scotch-Irish emigration, however, did not come until after 1714. Already suffering because of harsh religious and economic conditions, the Scotch-Irish faced a series of disasters that made the thought of crossing a vast ocean to seek a better life in an unknown environment seem like a very good idea. The most severe catastrophe was a lengthy drought that started in 1714 and lasted for six years, ruining crops, causing food prices to soar, and wiping out many small farmers. Two years later, misfortune struck again in the form of the disease known as "rot," which killed thousands of sheep. Then, in 1718, a smallpox epidemic raged throughout Ulster, causing more suffering and death.

In 1715, 300 people from Ulster petitioned Samuel Shute, the governor of New England, for a grant of land. The Reverend William Boyd, a Presbyterian minister from MaCosqin in County Londonderry crossed the Atlantic in 1718 to negotiate for the group. Upon his return, a small number of Scotch-Irish decided to emigrate to New England. For unknown reasons, Boyd and eleven other ministers who signed the petition did not go. Shortly thereafter, the Reverend James Woodside, another Presbyterian minister, led a second group, estimated at between 100 and 160 people. These emigrants left Londonderry in a boat named the *MacCullum* (or *McCollom*) and arrived in Boston in September 1718. A week after their arrival, they made their way to Maine, where they eventually found a hostile reception from the local Indians awaiting them.

During 1718, an estimated 1,000 people left the north of Ireland in ten vessels and made it to Boston. Though small in number, this migration had a significant effect. As Dickson says, these emigrants "showed tens of thousands of relations and friends they had left behind in the Bann and Foyle river valleys that, for ordinary people like themselves, life in America was a practical alternative to life in Ireland."[11] They led the way and established themselves, proving that it could be done.

From this small exodus began a continuous stream of emigration that continued unabated until the outbreak of the American Revolution. Although not all of the Irish were Scotch-Irish Presbyterians, the vast majority were. They left by droves from the five main ports of Ulster—Londonderry, Portrush, Belfast, Larne, and Newry—although some did leave from the southern ports of Dublin, Drogheda, and Sligo. By 1775, says the historian T. W. Moody, this emigration had "drained off many of the thousands of the most vigorous Presbyterians from Ulster."[12]

When life got tougher, more people left.[13] An analysis of the economic pattern shows that in addition to this initial wave, the tide was exceptionally strong in four other periods: 1722–28, 1740–41, 1754–55, and 1771–73. Each of these periods had its own spur to emigration—usually a combination of rack-renting, economic depression, famine, and disease. None of the five waves was directed toward any one region; the five periods of emigration benefited particular colonies at different times. "The first two helped fill up the back-country of Pennsylvania, and by 1730 the newcomers had already reached the northern part of the Shenandoah Valley of Virginia," Leyburn explains. "The third wave further peopled the Shenandoah and spread southward into the Piedmont and upcountry of North Carolina. That colony and South Carolina drew most of the immigrants in the fourth wave, while the final group, coming just before the Revolutionary War, spread out wildly from New York to Georgia."[14]

Almost from the beginning, officials in Dublin and England were alarmed at the migration. Since the overwhelming majority of the emigrants were Protestants, they were concerned that the loyal part of the population on which the government's strength depended would be seriously weakened. The greedy landowners were worried too, fearing that if too many people left, competition for the land would not be as great, rents would be reduced, and consequently so too would profits.

During the 1720s, reports indicate that the fears of the establishment were justified: the flow of people across the Atlantic was steadily increasing in volume. One Ulster minister wrote a friend in Scotland: "There is likely to be a great desolation in the northern parts of this kingdom by the removal of several of our brethren to the American plantations. No less than six ministers dismantled their congregations and great numbers of their people go with them."[15] In a letter written in 1728 to England's secretary of state, Archbishop Hugh Boulter described what he had seen: "It is certain that above 4200 men, women and children have been shipped within three years, and of these about 3100 last summer. The whole north is in ferment, and people everyday are engaging one another to go next year. The humor has spread like a contagious distemper and the people will hardly hear anyone who tries to cure them of their madness."[16]

By 1728 the migration, which had now reached 3,000 people a year, was causing a virtual panic among the ruling classes. Many complained that if the emigration rate continued, the entire Protestant population of Ulster would eventually find itself on the other side of the Atlantic. In a petition to the lord justices in Dublin, the Irish gentry expressed their fear of "a dangerous superiority of our inveterate enemy the papists, who openly and avowedly rejoice at this impending calamity and use all the means and artifices to encourage and persuade the Protestants to leave the nation and cannot refrain from boasting that they shall by those means have again all the lands of this kingdom in their possession."[17]

The Irish authorities finally decided to do something. In 1729 they appointed a commission to look into the causes of emigration; however, no action resulted from the investigation. Although there were many vocal expressions of concern at the loss of Protestants to the other British colonies, no concrete measures were ever introduced to stem the tide. One bill, designed to put some legal obstacles in the path of the emigrant, was eventually introduced before the Irish Parliament, but it was presented during a time of reduced emigration and was defeated.

The number of people who left Ireland is quite impressive considering the trip that had to be made. Leaving one's home behind forever and heading across the vast expanse of the Atlantic was quite a step; many problems had to be overcome before the emigrant could realize the dream of starting a new life in America. The first difficulty was to find the means to pay for the transatlantic voyage. While £10 may not seem like a large sum of money to us today, it was to a man in Ulster who for several years had been trying to support his family in the face of harsh economic conditions and the cruelty of nature. Not only did he have to find the money to pay for the passage, but additional funds were needed to purchase land, tools, and seed and to have enough to live on until at least the first harvest. Finding someone to pay the way was the only hope that many had. Thus, a large majority of the emigrants were those who received free passage in return for enduring a period of contracted service once they landed.

This practice known as indenturing was common throughout the colonial period, but no other ethnic group made use of it like the Scotch-Irish. During the course of the Scotch-Irish immigration, an estimated 100,000 came to America as indentured servants. Indenturing to pay a passage could work in two ways. The most common way was to sign a contract agreeing to serve the master of a ship or his assignee for an agreed period of time, usually four to seven years. Or the emigrant could agree to pay the cost of the passage within a short time after arriving in America in the hope that enough money could be raised either through the help of friends or by indenturing on the best terms available.

In the latter case, unable to raise the money within the agreed time, the emigrant would then be treated as an indentured servant and his or her services would be sold to the highest bidder. When the ships landed in America, advertisements for the sale of indentures would appear in the newspapers. One typical ad that appeared in the Charleston newspaper read: "Just imported here to be sold ... Irish servants, men and women, of good trades, from the north of Ireland, Irish linen, household furniture, butter, cheese, chinaware and all sorts of dry goods."[18]

During indenture, the colonist was fed, clothed, and housed. Once the term expired, the servant was given the means to begin a new life, normally money, tools, and in some instances, even cattle and weapons. Pennsylvania was particularly generous, giving the emigrant two suits of clothes, an ox, grubbing and weeding hoes, and fifty acres of land.

Today we might compare the lot of the indentured servant unfavorably to that of a slave or convict, but most of the indentured servants did not look at their situation that way. They saw it as a temporary loss of freedom, giving them the opportunity to escape the depressed and miserable living conditions in Ireland. As a newcomer in a strange environment, they were able to gain some experience and to learn the ways of the New World before setting out on their own.

The majority did not reach the status of Charles Thomson, who left his hometown of Maghera, County Londonderry, as an indentured servant and eventually became secretary of the Continental Congress, but many were able to buy land and, within a few years, be better off than they had been in Ireland. Because indentured servants were important to the success of the colonial enterprise, laws were enacted giving them rights and providing protection. The consent of the justice of the peace was needed, for example, before a servant could be punished. If too severely punished, the servant had the legal right to demand his or her freedom.

This is not to say that the life of an indentured servant was an easy one. If indentured to a cruel master, the servant could still be subjected to such abuses as whipping or branding. If punished for a crime, the servant could get up to seven years added to the term. But the indenture appeared to be an attractive alternative to the harsh conditions of the old country—so attractive, in fact, that some emigrants who had sufficient means to make it on their own indentured themselves in order to gain valuable experience.

The pull of the New World proved to be so irresistible that the indentured class included people from all walks of life, not only farmers and unskilled workers but also professional people and all kinds of tradesmen, such as carpenters, smiths, weavers, bricklayers, and shoemakers. Convicts were also indentured, but they formed a small part of the emigration to the American colonies. Although laborers were badly needed, many of the colonies, such as the provincial assembly of Virginia, passed laws restricting or prohibiting altogether the importation of convict labor. With time, more and more free Irish and Germans emigrated to America, and the need for indentured convicts decreased.

Whereas economic conditions in Ulster provided the initial stimulus to emigration, a number of other factors helped to keep the transatlantic migration flowing. The emigrants, once settled, began to send letters back home to friends and relatives, describing their new life. Many letters gave glowing accounts: the cheap and abundant land; the chance to better oneself for those not afraid of hard work; the favorable treatment; and the fact that a man could practice his religion without many restrictions. Some letters, of course, were probably written by emigrants who were actually unhappy but did not want those back home to think that they had made a mistake in coming to America. But it appears that most of the letters were written by settlers who were enthralled with their new environment and the opportunities it presented in comparison with Ireland. And when an emigrant's lot described in a letter happened to be an unhappy one, the shipmasters and colonial officials did not hesitate to censure the letters to make sure that unfavorable accounts did not make their way back to Ireland. Many letters were printed, with the blessing of government officials, in the newspapers and other publications of the day, persuading others to emigrate to the "Land of Promise" even in times when the pressures of poverty had been relieved.

By the middle of the eighteenth century, another inducement—newspaper advertisements placed by shipping agents—became an important way of encouraging emigration. Many of the ads included an addendum that extolled the virtues of the New World. One, announcing the voyage of the *Hopwell*, which sailed from Londonderry to Nova Scotia in 1766, was typical: "It would swell the advertisement to no great length to enumerate all the blessings those people enjoy who have already removed from this country to said province. It may suffice to say, that from tenants [they have] become landlords, from working for others they [are] now working for themselves, and enjoy the fruits of their own industry.[19]

Besides the shipping agent, who played an important role in transoceanic trade in emigrants, there eventually appeared another kind of agent, the land promoter, who was interested not in making money from the safe transportation of the emigrants to America but in finding people who were willing to come as colonists and settle anywhere from Nova Scotia to Florida. Being a land promoter was much more difficult than being a shipping agent. The land promoters had to find people with enough money to establish themselves as farmers in America, which was no easy task. The shipping agent, on the other hand, could concentrate on the great mass of the Scotch-Irish who did not have money and who might be even too poor to buy a ticket. In addition, emigrants recruited by a land promoter had no real choice in where they could settle. They had to go where the promoter's land was located, even if they did not particularly like the area. In comparison, the shipping agent had the advantage of offering emigrants passage to any part of America and giving them the choice of settling anywhere from Halifax to Savannah.

With a few exceptions, land promoting was rare in the first half of the eighteenth century, but the activity increased in the period from 1750 to the outbreak of the Revolutionary War. One of the first and the most prominent of the land promoters during this period was Arthur Dobbs, a wealthy landowner from County Antrim. After a distinguished career as high sheriff of the county, member of the Irish Parliament, and engineer-in-chief and surveyor-general of Ireland, Dobbs turned his attention to the American colonies. In 1745 he purchased 4000 acres from the McCollough estate, which was located in the present-day North Carolina counties of Cabarrus and Mecklenburg. Dobbs also received a grant of 60,000 acres in New Hanover County.

At first Dobbs paid little attention to his vast American landholdings because another project—the search for the Northwest Passage—consumed his time. But in 1747 he wrote Mathew Rowan, North Carolina surveyor-general, of his plan "to take a trip to Carolina and to take over some tenants ... and servants to settle them there and see the country."[20] Dobbs then became very active in seeking out Irish tenants for his land, even offering to pay them passage money. He had to be very aggressive because the terms of his grant stated that if any land had been planted that held fewer than one white settler per two hundred acres by 1775, that land would revert back to the Crown.

Dobbs personally knew many of those with whom he contracted, which explains why Dobbs, unlike most of the promoters who followed him, was considerate and kind toward those he brought to America. The first tenants for Dobbs' land arrived in 1751, and four years later, Dobbs came to the colonies to inspect his land, apparently not bringing many families with him. Of the seventy-eight families that were settled on his estates by the summer of 1755, no more than eighteen had come directly from the north of Ireland. Not until 1768—three years after the death of Dobbs—did the colony receive any more settlers.

Thomas Desbrisny and Alexander McNutt, both of whom operated after 1755, were more typical land promoters. Desbrisny was a shady character who used illegal practices to secure settlers for St. James Island (now known as Prince Edward Island). In glowing accounts published in the *Belfast Newsletter*, he misrepresented living conditions on the island. The amount of effort Desbrisny put into his venture did not equal the number of settlers he eventually recruited—9 families in 1771, 188 in 1772, and an undetermined but small number in 1773, significant in comparison with the volume of emigration for those years. After 1773, Desbrisny abandoned his efforts, mortgaging his land on St. James Island to a Dublin merchant named Drumond. Those who had purchased deeds from Desbrisny at first paid exorbitant rents and then eventually lost both their money and their land.

Although Alexander McNutt offered more favorable terms of settlement than any other land promoter of the colonial period, he proved to be an impractical dreamer. After some success in bringing about 400 to 500 emigrants to Nova Scotia in 1761 and 1762, he presented an ambitious proposal to the English government to transport an additional 7,000 to the province. Even though the plan was approved by the board of trade, the privy council became alarmed at the loss of such a large number of loyal Protestants and directed the colonial government to Nova Scotia "not to grant lands or to permit any of his majesty's subjects from Ireland to become settlers in that province except as such as have been residents in Nova Scotia or some part of his majesty's colonies in America for the space of five years."[21]

On the whole, emigration through land-promotion schemes proved unsuccessful. Hundreds, rather than thousands, left Ireland in this manner. Although tempted with offers of cheap passage, the use of livestock, and the help and friendship of established settlers, an emigrant still needed the money to survive at least a year and to purchase seeds and implements to cultivate the land. The average emigrant preferred to play it safe and to go to more familiar parts of America where friends and relatives were already settled.

If the emigrant somehow managed to find the means to pay for the ocean crossing, there was still the voyage itself with which to contend. It was a risky, terrifying, and dangerous trip, even for those who felt they had little to lose. The Atlantic was known for its severe weather and violent storms. Many of the ships were crowded, which increased the likelihood of disease. If the shipowner was negligent, or the trip took too long, food and water might become dangerously short. Sometimes the captain would skimp on the food to increase his profits.

In many instances, the problems of the emigrant began even before the ship set sail. Delays in departure were common, and there was no guarantee that the notice in the change of sailing date would be advertised. Sometimes captains would lie to their passengers, telling them that some of the other passengers had requested a delay in order to have more time to put their affairs in order. Often vessels would arrive on time but, in periods of stiff competition, the captain would wait, hoping to get his full complement of passengers.

The emigrants, many of whom had come from far away, might have to wait several weeks. To cite one example, the departure of a ship named the *Hopewell* was advertised to sail to Charleston from Belfast on August 5, 1772, but the sailing was postponed until August 28. Assurances were given that the vessel would arrive from America any day. After another delay, which lasted until September 15, the ship finally arrived. Still, two more "final" notices appeared before the ship set sail in the third week of October.

Delays meant hardships, since the emigrant would have to provide for himself and his family until the ship sailed. Lengthy delays most likely meant spending one's stake—the money needed to get a new start in America. Some historians have even suggested that shipmates deliberately postponed the departure date in the anticipation that people would spend their money, thereby reducing them to a penniless state. At the mercy of the shipowners, the emigrant would then be forced into becoming an indentured servant or returning home.

Once the voyage got under way, the emigrant could look forward to at least eight to ten weeks on the high seas and sometimes longer if conditions were unfavorable, or if Charleston or Savannah in the southern colonies was the destination and not a closer, more northern part. There is even a record of one ship that took five months to cross the Atlantic. If the ship was delayed or the voyage took longer than usual, starvation was a likely possibility, since it became customary for shipmasters to provide passengers with their full allowance of provisions from the advertised sailing date, whether or not the ship had actually set sail.

The ships carried an average of 120 to 140 people, who brought on board what personal possessions they could carry. The emigrants' quarters were usually cramped and overcrowded, especially during periods of heavy immigration. Living conditions were often made worse because many vessels were not designed to carry passengers. Adding to the space problem was the fact that in the eighteenth century, the Irish and British authorities had no restrictions on the number of passengers in relation to the berth space.

Colonial authorities, however, were quick to realize that overcrowded ships led to disease that might be brought into their province. Consequently, some provincial assemblies passed laws requiring a minimum amount of berth space per passenger. In 1749, for instance, the Pennsylvania assembly passed an act requiring the berth space for passengers to be "6 feet long and 118 inches wide, though space could be used to accommodate passengers who were less than 14 years of age."[22] The act, however, made little difference because it did not specify the height to be left between a berth and the one above it.

Although the Irish emigration trade in the eighteenth century experienced a high mortality rate as a result of the poor travel conditions, it appears that the Scotch-Irish fared much better than some of their European counterparts. This was especially true of the Germans who were coming to America during the same period. Some of the German ships, for example, were so ravaged by typhoid in the ocean crossing that in the emigrant trade, the disease became known as Palatine fever.

In times of bad weather or if smallpox, fever, or some other disease broke out, the passenger was confined below deck. In fact, much of the passenger's time was spent below deck, which meant a miserable experience. As Dickson points out, the emigrants not only slept below deck but also "ate and washed in bad weather, sang and wept, chafed under and obeyed the petty tyrants in their midst, and rejoiced for the newly born and mourned for the dead."[23] In addition to overcrowding and disease, ventilation and portholes to provide air were usually nonexistent in the emigration vessels of the period.

If a ship did survive the rough seas of the Atlantic but became shipwrecked in the process, this meant certain death for the passengers. What lifeboats there were on board usually consisted of a longboat and a yawl. The passengers were regarded merely as a kind of freight. Fortunately, very few emigrant ships from Ulster were lost at sea; in fact, there are only three recorded incidents of such mishaps.

One other peril facing emigrants should be mentioned: the prospect of encountering pirates, who were considered such a threat by Irish authorities that well into the second half of the eighteenth century, ships leaving Cork sailed under the protection of a convoy. Although there is no recorded capture of a northern Irish ship by pirates, the exploits of the privateers were often described in the Irish newspapers, causing much alarm among both the authorities and the general population.

If passengers managed to survive all of this—and the majority did—one more obstacle might await them at arrival at port. If they had not paid for their passage or signed an indenture with a colonial employer, they had to wait on board ship until the captain sold their labors to recoup the cost of their passage. The wait often meant little food or water and a chance of catching a disease.

Despite all the risks and hardships of the voyage, the Scotch-Irish continued to travel to America by the thousands. The tide increased again in 1740, when Ireland was once more at the mercy of harsh climatic conditions. The winter of 1739–40 proved to be one of the most severe in the century. In Ulster it was known as "the time of the black frost" because of the darkness of the ice and the lack of sunshine. The severe weather ruined the potato crop and caused famine all over Ireland, with an estimated 400,000 people dying during this period. The catastrophe spurred another wave of emigration during the next decade.

With the outbreak of the French and Indian War in the 1750s, the tide slackened again. It even appeared that the Scotch-Irish exodus might finally be over. But then a number of economic factors led to the century's biggest emigration. In 1770 thousands of leases in the large County Antrim estate of the earl of Donegall expired, and once again rack-renting was rampant. The rents were so greatly increased that many people could not pay and were subsequently evicted from farms that their families had owned for years. Groups of disgruntled tenants organized themselves under the name of the Hearts of Steel and tried to regulate the rents in the local districts, but the government sent troops to reestablish the status quo. Violent disturbances and pitched bottles ensued. Once again, faced with repression and a bleak future, thousands decided to take their chances and sail west. They were joined by victims of the declining linen industry. By 1773, linen production in the north had fallen between one-third and one-half, while linen prices fell one-fourth. Figures on the number of people emigrating during the 1770s range from 15,000 to 42,000.

By the beginning of the American Revolution, Scotch-Irish emigration had reached its peak. Since no adequate statistics exist in either Great Britain or America for population and immigration during the colonial period, it is difficult to tell just how many did emigrate. Records are fragmentary, and figures do not always agree. The most common figure cites 200,000 Scotch-Irish emigrants, although some historians have put it higher, even as high as 300,000. Leyburn says that it is "safe to say that considerably more than a quarter of a million Americans in 1790 had Scotch-Irish ancestry. Certainly this element, next to English, was the largest nationality group in the country."[24] If Leyburn is correct, then by the time of the Revolutionary War one American out of every ten was Scotch-Irish.

Emigration came to an abrupt halt when the news of the firing at Lexington and Concord reached Ireland in the summer of 1775. The colonies were now at war with the mother country, and during the next eight years British ships, which had previously taken passengers to America, now carried guns, troops, and ammunition. It would be a mistake, though, to assume that Scotch-Irish emigration ended with the colonial period, as some historians have suggested.[25] The American Revolution proved to be nothing more than a temporary interruption, and within just one year after the signing of the Treaty of Versailles, 5,000 more Irish emigrants had crossed the Atlantic. The urge to emigrate proved to be just as strong after the Revolution as it had been before. An estimated 100,000 left for America in the three decades after 1783. The historian Wayland Dunaway states that up until 1820, Ireland was supplying two-thirds of the country's emigrants and that by 1835, it was still furnishing the bulk of the emigrants.[26]

What did change about the Irish emigrant trade in the post–Revolutionary War period was its character. The number arriving at America's shores as indentured servants decreased substantially. More people now paid their way. Professional people came, as well as some moderately well-to-do. The newspapers and reports of the period are replete with examples of the changing status of the Irish emigrant. One typical report referred to a ship named the *Rose*, which had left Sligo for Philadelphia with more than 200 passengers, "most of whom were persons of distinction, and some of our best artisans with their families."[27]

During the 1790s, political and not economic reasons provided the impetus to Scotch-Irish emigration to America. Many emigrants were caught up in the political discontent that led to the formation of the United Irishmen. For a brief period, many Scotch-Irish Presbyterians joined the Irish Catholic in common bond against the English. However, when the British crushed the 1798 rebellion, emigration for political motives ceased.

After 1800, Scotch-Irishmen appeared less adventuresome, and instead of heading inland like previous shiploads of countrymen, they tended to stay on the east coast and settle in the cities, particularly New York, Philadelphia, and Baltimore. Others went to live with their relatives and friends who had settled in such well established areas of the United States as Pennsylvania, Virginia and the Carolinas.

As was the case in the colonial period, British officials became worried about the effect that the emigration would have on Ireland. In 1803 the government passed the Passenger Act, which severely limited the number of passengers that ships could carry across the Atlantic. The purpose of the act was to make it unprofitable for shipowners to carry passengers to North America. Although efforts were made to evade the act, the number of Irish emigrants was drastically reduced and emigration continued at a much lower ebb. Ten years later, the War of 1812 further broke the flow.

In the years between the American Revolution and the War of 1812, perhaps as many as 100,000 people, most of them Scotch-Irish, had settled in America. By 1820, however, significant Scotch-Irish emigration was coming to an end. There would be another tidal wave starting in the 1840s, when the potato famine ravaged Ireland, but this time the emigrants would be predominantly Catholic and would come not from Ulster but from southern Ireland.

6

Settling the New Land

After 1683, Europe was constantly at war for more than thirty years, and emigration to America came almost to a standstill. But after the 1713 Treaty of Utrecht and the series of subsequent treaties that followed, a new era of peace was ushered in, lasting for more than three decades. For most of the period before 1783, English culture and institutions dominated the American colonies, the only exception being the Dutch in New York and the Huguenots in the South. During the following century, this ethnic homogeneity was shattered forever as a number of groups either migrated or were imported in such large numbers that by the time of the American Revolution, half of the colonial population south of New England was non-English. Germans, Africans, Swiss, Swedes and Jews all came, but the largest group to make the transatlantic migration was the Scotch-Irish.

The Scotch-Irish first sought refuge in New England, where on the surface, at least, they appeared to have a lot in common with the local inhabitants. Like the New Englanders, the Scotch-Irish were Puritan in religion and had emigrated to America because of religious persecution. Some of the more prominent New Englanders even encouraged Scotch-Irish settlement because they were worried by the Indian threat and believed that if the Scotch-Irish could be induced to come and settle on the frontier, the newcomers would make an excellent buffer between potential trouble and the established settlements.

After a small group of Scotch-Irish landed in Boston in 1713 and settled in Worcester, a slight trickle followed during the next six years, leading to small settlements along the western shore of the Connecticut River in what is today Vermont, along the Kennebee River; on Casco Bay, Maine; and in southern New Hampshire. A look at a modern-day map of the region will quickly show such Ulster names as Coleraine in Massachusetts, Belfast in Maine, and Londonderry in New Hampshire and Vermont, indicating that some of these settlements took root.

Although the leaders in New England were receptive, most of the New England populace proved to be cold and indifferent to the Scotch-Irish arrival, and the immigrants soon found a hostile, bigoted, and intolerant environment similar to the one they had left behind in Ireland. The Puritan New Englanders simply did not like outsiders and were not interested in the plight of any people but their own. Today, we would call the Puritans snobs. To them, all newcomers were "unclean, unwholesome, and disgusting."[1] So wherever the Scotch-Irish settled in New England, they were made to feel uncomfortable.

Economics also played a factor in shaping the Puritan attitude. The Scotch-Irish arrival coincided with a rapid rise in the cost of living, causing the New Englander to worry about the expense of providing relief for strangers who, although poor, were not "one's own." Some New Englanders openly complained that "these confounded Irish will eat us all up."[2] This concern eventually reached hysterical proportions, and the Puritans became increasingly more aggressive in their efforts to discourage settlement. When one ship from Ireland landed in Boston in 1719, for example, its passengers were ordered to get out of town immediately. Four years later, an ordinance was passed requiring all Irish immigrants to register with the town clerk. In 1729 an angry mob went to Boston Harbor and prevented the landing of a ship from Londonderry.

This harassment continued into the 1730s, but by that time the Scotch-Irish had gotten the message, and immigration slowed considerably, allowing New England to preserve its essential homogeneity. Estimates indicate that Scotch-Irish emigration to this part of the colonies in the eighteenth century barely reached 20,000 people.

The Scotch-Irish began to look southward for more favorable places to settle. Although they eventually went to all thirteen colonies, most places had little to attract them in large numbers. To settle in New York, for instance, meant to try and improve one's lot under a system that favored large landowners over the small proprietor. Going to Virginia meant having to deal with a narrow religious policy, whereas another possibility, the seaboard of the Tidewater South, had a slaveowning plantation economy and an established church, which were alien to the background of the Scotch-Irish. New Jersey was definitely not the place for indentured servants to go; although this colony would later become one of the strongholds of Presbyterianism in America, it was the Scots and not the Scotch-Irish who made it so.

When the Scotch-Irish finally completed assessing their prospects in each of the colonies, they had no trouble in concluding that Pennsylvania offered the best opportunities. It is not difficult to understand why the Scotch-Irish were attracted to this colony, for Pennsylvania had much to offer—plenty of cheap, fertile land ready for the taking and enough game that one did not need to worry about going hungry, for starters. Compared with Ireland, the climate may have been colder in the winter and hotter in the summer, but it was a lot better than what some of their fellow countrymen were experiencing in New England. As for religion, the Pennsylvania charter made the colony one of the most tolerant places on earth. As R. J. Dickson explains, "In very few other parts of the world in the eighteenth century was any and every person who acknowledged God as the creator, upholder and ruler of the world free from religious persecution or prejudice and free from any obligation to attend and maintain a place of worship."[3]

Most encouraging was the warm welcome the Scotch-Irish received from the Quaker William Penn, the founder and namesake of Pennsylvania. Penn had received his charter in 1681, making

Pennsylvania one of the last of the original colonies to be founded, and in order to attract settlers, Penn had started an aggressive advertising campaign in which he used personal visits to Europe and the distribution of broadsides to publicize the colony's advantages.

At first he concentrated on recruiting members of minority sects who were suffering the type of persecution that the Quakers had long endured. Penn visited Germany and convinced large numbers of Dunkards, Mennonites, Amish, and members of other pietist sects to emigrate to Pennsylvania. To help finance and encourage settlement, Penn persuaded a number of leading sectarians to organize the Frankfurt Company. The first group from Germany came in 1683 and settled at what became Germantown, not far from Philadelphia. It took some time and a lot of hard work, but by 1708, the Germans began arriving in significant numbers, first stopping at Germantown before pushing on into the neighboring counties of Pennsylvania.

Penn wanted to attract other groups besides the Germans. He was particularly interested in the Scotch-Irish, whom he believed had the kind of qualities needed to develop the colony. He instructed his provincial secretary, James Logan, a Scotch-Irishman, to extend a welcome to his fellow countrymen. Logan, born in Lurgan near Belfast in 1674, had met Penn when involved in the shipping trade between Dublin and Bristol and accepted his invitation to be the provincial secretary of Pennsylvania. Logan arrived in Philadelphia in 1699 and received a large tract of land in present day Lancaster County, which he named Donegal after the Irish county of the same name.

After 1724, Philadelphia, New Castle, and other Delaware ports began taking the bulk of the Scotch-Irish. Some stayed in Delaware and a few others crossed the river into New Jersey and Maryland, but most went to Pennsylvania, where the first settlements took root in western Chester County. As more and more came, the Scotch-Irish began to spill into Lancaster County and the southern part of Dauphin County. When immigration began to increase considerably, it became impossible for this part of Pennsylvania to support all who came. Consequently, the Scotch-Irish began to move westward toward the Susquehanna and beyond, generation after generation motivated by the prospect of owning their own land and having the opportunity to make a mark on the world.

A look at a modern map of Pennsylvania will show the many Irish place-names marking the advance of the Scotch-Irish across the colony's landscape: Donegal (Lancaster, Westmoreland and Washington Counties), Londonderry (Dauphin, Chester, and Mifflin Counties), Denmore (Lancaster County), Antrim (Franklin County), Strabane (Adams County), Monaghan (York County), Tyrone (Perry and Blair Counties), Fermanagh (Juniata County), and Armagh (Mifflin County). So steady was the Scotch-Irish settlement of Pennsylvania that by the time of the American Revolution, the Scotch-Irish constituted one-third of its population.

Like the other immigrant groups that populated America, the Scotch-Irish sought out and settled among their own people, mixing little with their neighbors, the Germans. Religion, language, culture, custom, and appearance separated the two groups, and more than one contemporary noted their differences. The Germans were seen as considerate, law-abiding, cooperative, even tempered, and fair in their treatment of the Indians, whereas the Scotch-Irish were usually described as hot-tempered, rash, combative, and unfair toward the Indians. Neither the Germans nor the Scotch-Irish liked the other or wanted the other as neighbors. Although there were occasional flare-ups, particularly over property rights or at election time, they tended to avoid each other.

As both groups pushed into the interior, their paths of settlement remained peculiarly but consistently parallel. The Scotch-Irish would settle one part of the country and the Germans another. In describing the process, James Leyburn has said, "If it could have been viewed by some miraculous slow motion machine, [it] might have resembled the stately rhythm of a formal dance."[4] This dance culminated in one of the great frontier movements in history.

"Step by step," says Wayland Dunaway, "they advanced a long and perilous path, surmounting whatever difficulties arose, moving even further into the wilderness and reclaiming it a new civilization."[5] By the time of the American Revolution, less than sixty years after their arrival in America, the Germans and the Scotch-Irish had settled the valleys of Pennsylvania and Virginia and the Carolina Piedmont.

German emigration to the colonies during the first three-fourths of the seventeenth century was almost as large as the Scotch-Irish emigration, and though we are mainly concerned here with the history of the Scotch-Irish, it is important to note that the Germans also contribute much to the making of America. They proved to be practical people skilled in many arts and crafts, which they adopted to their needs, and are credited with giving the frontier the Kentucky rifle, the Conestoga wagon, the log cabin, and perhaps the covered bridge.

With time, the Pennsylvania authorities became happy with the more passive and cooperative Germans and began to worry about the increasingly large numbers of Scotch-Irish. In 1729 James Logan wrote, "We may easily believe that there are some grounds for the common apprehension of the people that if some speedy method be not taken, they [the Scotch-Irish] will make themselves proprietors of the province."[6] The next year he complained again, "A settlement of five families from Ireland gives one more trouble than fifty of any other people."[7]

It was not just the large numbers that disturbed the authorities. When Logan had invited the Scotch-Irish, he had actually thought they would be a leading example to others. He soon changed his mind, however, coming to the conclusion that the Scotch-Irish were a nuisance. What bothered Logan and the other colonial officials the most was the Scotch-Irish practice of squatting on land without securing legal title to it. As early as 1726 Logan complained, "There at this time [is] over a 100,000 acres possessed by persons, who resolutely sit down and improve, without any manner of Right or Pretence to it."[8]

The Scotch-Irish argued that "it was against the laws of God and nature that so much land should be idle when so many Christians wanted it to labor on and to raise their children."[9] They resisted all attempts to make them pay for the land or expel them. A few upstart Scotch-Irish even settled on Penn's own manor of Conestoga. Some thought it better to let the Scotch-Irish squat because if they were removed from the land, they might settle among the English and Germans, and trouble would result.

It would be misleading, however, to say that squatting was peculiar to the Scotch-Irish. Not surprisingly, the practice was common on the American frontier. Many arrivals had no money or were too poor to buy land, even though prices were cheap. Besides, why buy land when one could move just a little farther west and get it for nothing? The authorities, at a loss to solve the problem, burned down the squatters' cabins and tried to intimidate them by sending out sheriffs or other law officials. But there were too many squatters and not enough colonial officials to control the situation. No sooner did the authorities leave than the squatters would come right back.

What worried Penn and the Quakers most about squatting was the danger it posed to the good-neighbor policy they had adopted toward the Indians. They went to extraordinary pains to get along with the natives, even going so far as to not allow a white man in the region before he had purchased the land from the Indians. It was not long before the impatient and ambitious Scotch-Irish started to come into conflict with the rights of Indians, who complained but to no avail. As more and more Indian land was taken illegally, resentment swelled and clashes became more frequent. It would not be long before a full-scale war would rage across the frontier.

By 1730, the Scotch-Irish were filling the part of the Cumberland Valley that today comprises Cumberland and Franklin Counties. This settlement increased in momentum during the next decade, encouraged by the authorities, who were willing to make land available at cheap prices in the hope that the Scotch-Irish would serve as a protective barrier against the Indians and as a means of guarding the southern border of the province against the intrusion of Marylanders. Dunaway described the Cumberland Valley "as the headquarters of the Scotch-Irish not only in Pennsylvania but in America as well ... the seed-plot and nursery of their race, the original reservoir, which after having been filled to overflowing, sent forth a constant stream of emigrants to the northward and especially to the South and West."[10] He estimated that by 1750, the Scotch-Irish composed about 90 percent of the population of the Cumberland Valley, with the Germans and English making up the other ten.[11]

Settlers began reaching the foothills of the Alleghanies by the mid-1730s and had two choices if they wanted to push on: either cross the mountains into western Pennsylvania or move southward into the Shenandoah Valley of Virginia and then into the Piedmont of the Carolinas. The latter was more appealing, since moving south was easier than attempting to cross a rugged mountain barrier. Government policy also discouraged settlement of western Pennsylvania. No land was offered for sale in this region before the Land Purchase of 1768, and no adequate military protection was available for the settlers' safety.

In the nearly 125 years after the founding of Jamestown, Virginia had become a plantation colony, dominated by the Tidewater gentry. By the beginning of the eighteenth century, however, its colonial government was eager to encourage the settlement of the backcountry to provide a buffer against possible Indian attacks. To spur settlement, Virginia initiated a policy of granting large tracts of land to speculators. John and Isaac Van Meter, for example, received 40,000 acres—a grant that included much of the three modern-day counties of Frederick and Clarke in Virginia and Jefferson in West Virginia. While some who settled were Scotch-Irish, most were Germans.

Two large grants brought the Scotch-Irish streaming into the southern and central part of the valley. The first gave William Beverly, John Robinson, and John and Richard Randolph a little over

118,000 acres of land. The grant, which covered the northern part of present-day Augusta County including the cities of Waynesboro and Staunton, was soon taken over by Beverly individually and became known as the "Beverly Grant."

The second grant, issued three months later, gave Benjamin Borden of New Jersey 500,000 acres, embracing most of modern-day Rockbridge County and the southern part of Augusta County. Before receiving title, Borden had to have one hundred families settled on the tract. He met the requirement and received title in 1739. By 1746 Borden's land had attracted so many Scotch-Irish settlers that it became known as the "Irish Tract."[12]

Beverly and Borden made the southern end of the Valley of Virginia the second great center for Scotch-Irish settlement after southeastern Pennsylvania, and up until the American Revolution, a steady number of Scotch-Irish settlers poured into the region, giving the area the highest concentration of Scotch-Irish in the colonies. "Nowhere in America today," says Dunaway, "are the Scotch-Irish more strongly entrenched or their influence more clearly seen than Augusta and Rockbridge counties, Virginia. Educationally, this influence manifested itself in the founding of Washington University (later Washington and Lee University), which has been termed the Scotch-Irish University of the South, while, religiously, it made this district one of the strongholds of Presbyterianism."[13]

Eventually, this region became not just a place of settlement but also a springboard for further migration to the Carolinas, Georgia, Tennessee, Kentucky, and parts farther west. The Shenandoah Valley of Virginia became the great highway used by increasing numbers of settlers looking for new land. It became famous as part of the Great Wagon Road extending from Philadelphia to Augusta, Georgia—a distance of about six hundred miles in all. A constantly shifting frontier became the norm in this southward migration. Those who had bought land and developed it could make a large profit by selling to latecomers and, with their profits, could then move onto the fringes of the frontier and buy large tracts of cheap land.

Settlers from Pennsylvania began reaching North Carolina by 1740 and continued to come at a steady rate up until the Revolution. The Scotch-Irish composed the largest single group, but there were also some English, Welsh, and Quakers. North Carolina governors Gabriel Johnston, Matthew Rowan, and Arthur Dobbs encouraged this emigration because they needed people to help develop the province. Most of the Scotch-Irish settled in the present-day counties of Granville, Rowan, Orange, Mecklenburg, Guilford, Davidson, Cabarrus, and in the extreme northwest part of the colony. The growth rate was so phenomenal that by the Revolutionary War, the population of North Carolina stood at about 83,000.

Movement and settlement across the ever-shifting frontier continued at a peaceful pace until 1755, when a bloody war erupted between the whites and the Indians. Known as the French and Indian War, the conflict lasted for more than seven years, putting a stop to immigration from Ireland and breaking the rhythm of the "Great Migration." It was an inevitable development, for the settlers, particularly the Scotch-Irish, had continued to encroach into Indian territory despite the efforts of colonial officials. Clashes had become more frequent, making it extremely difficult to keep the peace.

On March 16, 1752, Richard Peter, secretary of the province, wrote, "The trespassers beyond the hills still continue, they are considerably increased and it is an exceeding embarrassment to know what to do."[14] The Indians became the allies of the French, who promised that if the English were defeated, the Indians would get back the land that had been taken from them. In 1755, the Indians broke loose with a vengeance upon frontier settlements extending from Canada to southern Virginia.

Although the fighting that occurred in Pennsylvania's frontier region was fierce, the colony's Quaker government made hardly any defensive preparations and even showed a reluctance to commit arms and men to deal with the crisis. The Quakers were safe in the East, away from the frontier and the scene of the hostilities, and did not care about the settlers' plight. The provincial secretary wrote in disgust: "In the midst of all this misery, the citizens are doing their business as usual, without much seeming concern. They neither muster, arm, nor fortify, nor make one effort for the relief of the back inhabitants."[15] Despite the massacres, the defeats, and the desire of most of the people to fight, the Pennsylvania general assembly, which was controlled by the Quakers, held firm. The situation became so desperate, however, that the colonial governor took matters into his own hands and declared war in 1756.

The Scotch-Irish settlements were nearest the Indians, and they bore the brunt of the Indian onslaught. The settlers soon learned that to have any chance at all, they would have to abandon traditional methods and adopt the Indian ways. They proved more than capable, matching the Indians savagery for savagery, killing for killing, and atrocity for atrocity. The tactics of both sides made for a vicious war. One Frenchman wrote about the Indians: "It is incredible what a quantity of scalps they bring us. These miserable English are now in the extremity of distress."[16] The Scotch-Irish took a few scalps themselves as they organized into bands of rangers and carried surprise attacks deep into Indian territory, where they burned villages and even killed women and children. Everyone in the Scotch-Irish settlement helped in its defense, even the ministers, who fought alongside their congregations, often preaching with their guns beside them in the pulpit.

The intensity of the fighting forced many whites to flee the Valley of Virginia for the safety of the Carolinas. "In one week of October 1756," wrote the historian Carl Bridenbaugh, "three hundred persons went by Belford Court House (in Virginia) on their way to Carolina and five thousand more had crossed James River, only at one ferry, that is Goodland Courthouse."[17]

The tide of battle did not turn until 1758, when the English captured Fort Duquesne, forcing the French to abandon their stronghold, the Ohio River valley. By 1760 Canada was in the hands of the English; three years later, the French surrendered.

The Indians had lost their allies, but they refused to give up and made one last concerted attempt for victory. No sooner had the French and English signed the peace treaty than the Indians, friend and foe alike, joined together under Chief Pontiac for a massive assault on the frontier settlements.

The Indians attacked with a fury. In Pennsylvania alone, two thousand whites died; in Virginia a whole settlement was massacred. Farms were devastated, crops ruined. Many settlers living on the frontier fled their homes for the refuge of older settlements. Hostilities ceased only after two successful expeditions into the Ohio Valley finally crushed the Indian alliance.

Pontiac's defeat marked a turning point in American history. With the Indian enemy decisively defeated, the white settlers now stood in complete control of the frontier. They could once again continue the march southward on through the Valley of Virginia into the Carolinas. With no physical barriers to prevent their movement, and with the Indians no longer a threat, the Scotch-Irish began pushing beyond North Carolina into the South Carolina Piedmont in the region between the Pee Dee (Yadkin) and Catawba Rivers. This area, known as the Waxhaws, became a kind of central distribution point from which settlers moved into the modern-day counties of Lancaster, York, Chester, Fairfield, Union, Newberry, Abbeville, and Edgefield.

The South Carolina authorities also induced Irish emigrants to come directly from Ireland, offering attractive bounties of one hundred acres per man and fifty acres per woman and child and the necessary farm implements to get started. Charleston now replaced New York as the second-most-important port of destination for emigrant ships from Ireland, although most of South Carolina's settlers continued to come from Pennsylvania, Maryland, and Virginia via the Great Wagon Road. By the time of the Revolutionary War, an estimated 60,000 were living in the colony.

The 1763 Treaty of Paris eventually led to a significant shift in the direction of the movement of people on the frontier. Soon, settlers would press into the trans-Allegheny region of the Ohio

Valley and the territory south of it, the vast tract of land ceded by the French to the English. No longer would settlement be restricted west of the mountains to the region extending from Pennsylvania to Georgia. The English authorities, however, delayed settlement by issuing a royal proclamation in 1763 that attempted to set up a boundary line to prevent further trouble between the whites and the Indians.

A substantial number of pioneers crossed the mountains into southwestern Pennsylvania beginning in 1779 when the land office opened for the sale of lands in the "New Purchase" of 1768. In the first month, over thirty-two thousand applications for warrants were made, many by Scotch-Irish who had come from southeastern Pennsylvania, especially the Cumberland Valley, or directly from Ireland in the large exodus of 1771–73.

It was not until after the Revolutionary War, when the English were no longer around to curb settlement, that the great push across the mountains began. Once again, the old desire for new land and better opportunities resurrected itself. Thousands of settlers moved into western Pennsylvania, Kentucky, Tennessee, and Ohio. By 1890 Pittsburgh had become a flourishing town and an active center for settlers on their way to the Ohio Valley.

It was a new chapter in the frontier history. The Scotch-Irish would play a major role in settling the west, but they were not the same type of people who had earlier been instrumental in opening up the frontier as it shifted from Maine to South Carolina. The Scotch-Irish, like other pioneers, no longer thought of themselves as a member of an ethnic group or as settlers from a particular area, and they began to interact to a degree that was unknown east of the mountains. One's origins or birthplace was no longer important; the Scotch-Irish had become Americans.

In describing this change, Leyburn has written: "There was nothing like the familiar concentration of Scotch-Irish in one neighborhood and Germans in another settlement that took place in the east…. On the contrary, there was the intermingling and intermarriage of people that is now a characteristic of the American people."[18] The Scotch-Irish, the people who had played such an important role in opening up the frontier, were now, in Leyburn's words, "the subject of historians and antiquarians."[19]

7

Life on the Frontier

When the Scotch-Irish arrived in America and set out for the frontier, much hardship and struggle awaited them before they could better their position. Frontier life proved to be a constant challenge that required much optimism, self-reliance, and fortitude. Just the task of traveling to one's destination was dangerous and difficult, for most of the roads were in poor condition and barely passable— full of holes, bogs, stumps, and fallen timbers. The journey was slow; settlers had to travel on horseback and used packhorses to transport their goods, and it was not until after the Revolution that wagons came into particular use.

On arrival, the settlers could not afford to waste time. Land had to be cleared and crops planted. They were constantly on guard against the threat of Indian attack, but they observed the native ways and learned a great deal, adopting the Indians' methods of hunting and of clearing the forest and absorbing the Indians' vast store of knowledge about plants, animals, and forest lore. Indian corn became a prolific substitute for oats and barley, providing food for both the settler's family and his animals, while other Indian crops, such as squash, beans, pumpkin, and sweet potatoes, were added to the frontiersman's diet. He even began to look like a native, dressing in the Indian-style clothing of deerskin shirt and moccasins and wearing his hair long, like the Indian, dressing it with bear's grease and tying it with an eel skin or leather whang.

Almost from the beginning, the log house or log cabin, as it came to be called, became the Scotch-Irish settler's principal type of dwelling. The Swedes who had first settled on the Delaware were probably the first builders of log cabins, but it was a German version that the Scotch-Irish adopted.[1] The early log cabins were built using the timber from the cleared fields. They consisted of a single room, usually with a loft above. This was an all-purpose building, serving as sitting room, kitchen, workplace, living room, bedroom, and in many cases, a place for some of the livestock to live. The pioneer mother cooked on a wide-open hearth, located in the center of the house and amply fitted with a crane and iron pots, flesh-hooks and pothooks, griddles and frying pans. The cabin was simply furnished; everything was homemade.

The historian Wayland Dunaway notes, "After the second generation reached maturity, house-raising became a standardized and regular organized activity on the frontier."[2] On this festive occasion, the neighbors would come to lend a hand; the men worked hard, the children played outdoors, and the women prepared a big meal. The cabin took about a day to be raised.

Once the frontiersman had built a roof over his head, the arduous task of clearing the land could begin. The settler relied on his principal tool, the ax, to clear the forests, which were thick with trees and shrubs. This slow process took several years. The Scotch-Irish, like the Indians, did not clear the stumps. Instead, they preferred to make fresh clearings and move on once they had "taken the good out of the land."[3] It was a wasteful method that utilized no crop rotation or soil conservation. The farms, often located on the side of hills or gaps, allowed the settlers to practice the type of grazing they had known in Ireland.

Eventually, land clearing became standardized, accomplished by log rollings in which the neighbors would come to help. These "logging bees" might clear several acres in a day. When the task was finally completed, farming could begin. All work in the fields involved the hardest manual labor. Methods were crude and implements primitive. For a long period, the settlers had no wagons to pull heavy loads. Instead, sleds became the main means of hauling material, even during the summer.

Since settlements were scattered, the frontier family had to be totally self-sufficient. For most of the time, especially in the colonial period, the family lived an isolated existence. Poor roads, almost impassable in the winter, made communications with the more settled parts infrequent and difficult.

With little money in circulation, bartering became the common method of exchanging goods and services. Certain commodities had a standardized value for trade purposes. Salt, for example, was scarce and therefore valuable. Bartering continued until after the Revolution, and in some parts of northwest Pennsylvania, a barter economy was still in operation until after 1840.

Relying on their own resources, the settlers became jack-of-all-trades who learned how to build their own furniture, shoe their own horses and make their own shoes.[4] Each family had a spinning wheel, which was used to make practically all of the family's clothes. The Scotch-Irish developed considerable skill at woodworking and learned how to make knives, bowls, troughs, mallets, and other utensils.

As skilled hunter, the settler used his gun to hunt bear, rabbits, squirrel, deer, or whatever wild game was available to keep his larder filled with meat. He also fished the mountain streams and gathered wild fruit when in season. Bee trees were plentiful, and the frontiersman quickly learned how to gather wild honey. It was common for a family to have a garden, which provided a variety of wholesome vegetables.

The wife and children were expected to work and to do their share. For the wife, who organized the household's domestic economy, the duties were many. She did the cooking, washing, and sewing; made and mended the clothes; milked the cows and churned the butter; baked the bread, often after grinding the meal herself; raised the children and taught them to read and the principles of Christianity; took care of family members when they were sick; gathered nuts, herbs, and fruits from the forest; and helped defend the home from Indians and wild animals, often when the husband was away. It was a hard life. In describing the life of the wife and mother, Dunaway says, "Her life was a ceaseless round of household duties and domestic chores, of loneliness and drudgery, often resulting in wearing herself out and becoming prematurely old."[5]

Idleness would not be the children's lot. From an early age, the boys would help their fathers in the fields, while the girls would work alongside their mothers in the house. What they learned from their parents would help them later when they married and had their own farms.

Although for the most part the frontiersman spent most of his time struggling to eke out an existence, he still made time for recreation and diversion. The activities that the men enjoyed were very physical, often rough, and even violent at times. Some of the favorite sports were fishing, foot-racing, jumping, hunting, shooting at marks, and throwing a tomahawk. Work and pleasure were often the same thing and made a good excuse for socializing. When families got together, the men would join in wood-choppings, logrollings, house-raisings, and corn-huskings while the women would organize quilting parties.

In the wintertime, when there was a lull in farming activities and the settler had more time to relax, he and his family would visit neighbors, if they were not too far away. The women brought the spinning wheel to pass the time, while the men talked about farming life. The visitors would usually stay until bedtime, which for the frontiersman was about nine o'clock in the evening.

Two special social occasions for the Scotch-Irish were weddings and funerals, both of which developed into ritualized customs. A volley of shots would usually begin the wedding day, followed by a mile-long run for the whiskey bottle by two of the area's best riders. The winner would take the bottle and pass it among the guests. The minister was the first to take a swig before performing the wedding. After all the men had a chance to kiss the bride, everyone sat down to a hearty dinner and they joined in an afternoon of fun and games.

The evening's festivities began with a big dance. Later at night, a ceremony was held, with the women leading the bride to her bed, followed by the men with the groom. When both were in bed, the couple was saluted with a loud serenade beat out on pots and pans.

The funeral ceremony resembled an Irish wake. Before being transported to its final resting place, the body lay at home, where the service took place. The friends and family sat up with the body through the night, praying and reading from the Scriptures. Before long, however, the atmosphere changed. As one observer recalled, "the glass with its exhilarating beverage would circulate freely, so that, before the dawn, the joke and the laugh, if not scenes more boisterous, would break upon the slumbers of the dead."[6]

Although whiskey was plentiful, drunkenness was not a common condition on the frontier. "Character and self-control revealed the man: sobriety (not abstention) distinguished itself from occasional drunkenness, and this in turn from 'drinking too much,'" Leyburn explains.[7] Dunaway further notes: "There was far less drinking on the frontier when compared to more settled parts such as eastern Pennsylvania. There, it became a common sight to see many young people drink themselves under the table at the local tavern or at weddings and funerals."[8]

Whiskey drinking was not confined to special occasions such as wedding celebrations and funeral ceremonies. It was an important part of every social occasion, whether large or small. Stills abounded on the frontier as the pioneers quickly learned to adapt their new crop, corn, into whiskey. In Scotch-Irish communities, ministers were invited to drink along with their parishioners, indicating that drinking was an accepted custom.

The frontiersmen thought that whiskey, if consumed in moderation, had a beneficial effect, especially as a means of promoting neighborliness and sociability. He also believed that whiskey had medicinal properties and was a good remedy for a number of diseases, including rheumatism and snake bites. Whiskey distilling also made good economic sense. Produced from surplus corn, it proved to be a good source of income and was easier to ship to market than bushels of grain.

As had been the case in Scotland and later in Ireland, the Presbyterian Church became the center of the Scotch-Irishman's life and the stern guardian of his morality. From an early age, the church assumed rigid control over the personal lives of its members. Leyburn describes the process: "Community control over wrong-doing began at an early age, when the child accompanied his parents to church, sat through the long services, learned the catechism and recited it to the minister, and witnessed the disciplining of church members. This implanted in his very being before he could effectively resist, his moral standards, like his conscience, was ingrained."[9] Everything in the community became the subject of church scrutiny: family arguments, violations of the Sabbath, fighting, swearing, and even cases involving the conduct of indentured servants.

During the colonial period, it was difficult to organize congregations and to find ministers to serve them. Appeals to the presbyteries and synods located in the more settled parts went largely unheeded. For a time the need was met by a circuit rider, a young clergyman who carried his meager belongings in a saddlebag and rode from one community to another, holding services in barns, in the open fields, or wherever a place could be found. These dedicated ministers had to travel over rough roads, often in bad weather. Their salaries were small; usually they were paid in kind rather than cash. To make ends meet, many ministers supplemented their income by teaching school in their homes.

With time, congregations became sufficiently large that a church was organized, a meetinghouse created, and a burial ground in the immediate vicinity laid out. Hot in the summer and cold in the winter, the churches of the colonial period were simple and plain, made of rough log structures. Frontier families would come from far distances to attend services, which became an all-day event, lasting from early in the morning to late at night. The service began with the minister delivering a long sermon, sometimes lasting up to ninety minutes, while the parishioners listened attentively. A long period of Scripture reading, praying, and hymn singing would follow.

During recess, people ate their lunch they had brought with them and socialized and gossiped with their fellow parishioners. Then another program of reading and praying began, lasting about three hours. The day's proceedings continued at a leisurely pace, for no one was in a great hurry. After all, the congregants had come a long way, and not often did they get the chance to talk with friends and neighbors about their families and life on the farm. As Dunaway has written, "A church meeting was an event in their lives, and they made the most of it."[10]

Buoyed by their strong faith in religion and exhibiting the determination, adaptability, and resourcefulness that had characterized their life in Ireland and Scotland, the Scotch-Irish proved successful in coping with the rugged conditions of their new environment. As the largest single group on the frontier, the Scotch-Irish played an influential role in molding the frontiers lifestyle. The settlements that they established became models for later settlers from other ethnic groups. They helped to popularize their adopted German-style log cabin in the West, and eventually, the dress and appearance of the eighteenth-century Scotch-Irish frontiersman became part of American folklore. Most important, the Scotch-Irish became a vanguard of the national movement that pressed forward, ever westward, and helped build the young American nation.

8

The Scotch-Irish and the Making of America

During the eighteenth century, the Scotch-Irish came to America by the thousands, the largest non-English ethnic group to emigrate before the Revolution. Although no exact figures exist, it is believed that perhaps as many as 250,000 Scotch-Irish, about one out of ten Americans, settled in the colonies. Their settlements stretched across the frontier, from Maine to Georgia. James Leyburn estimates that by the time of independence, Scotch-Irish communities numbered 70 in New England, from 30 to 40 in New York, 50 to 60 in New Jersey, 50 in North Carolina, and perhaps 70 in South Carolina and Georgia.[1] Because of their large numbers, the Scotch-Irish played an important role in the development of education, religion, and politics, in westward expansion, and in the events that led to the birth of the American nation.

As had been the case in Scotland and Ireland, religion shaped the lives of Scotch-Irish immigrants and influenced their involvement in colonial life. From the time of Calvin and Knox, the Scotch-Irish had been devout Presbyterians who had held firmly to their faith despite the Anglican policies of English officials. Churches were usually the first institutions established in America by the Scotch-Irish.

Francis Makemie, a minister who had immigrated to America in 1683 from County Donegal, Ireland, organized the first Presbyterian church in the colonies. Then, in 1706, he met with seven ministers from Maryland, Delaware, and Pennsylvania to form the New World's first Presbytery. By 1717, thirteen Presbyterian churches had been organized near Philadelphia. This figure doubled during the 1720s as churches sprang up in Pennsylvania and New Castle County, Delaware. The first was the so-called Rock Church, organized one mile from present-day Lewisville, Maryland, on the Pennsylvania border.

By the 1730s, the flood of Scotch-Irish immigrants was causing a big problem for the Presbyterian Church. There were simply more congregations than ministers who were willing to make a long, transatlantic sea voyage to settle in an unfamiliar land where the life was hard and the pay poor. Matters were made worse by the church's requirement for a highly educated clergy. Each Presbyterian minister had to be a university graduate who had undergone a rigorous training period, which included the study of Greek, Latin, and Hebrew. The Scottish universities, which trained the Presbyterian ministers, were few in number and could not supply enough to meet the demands of the congregations even in Ireland. Sometimes years of petitioning by a frontier settlement would be required before the appropriate Presbytery provided a minister.

To meet the need, schools began to open in the colonies, the first being the celebrated "Log College" of the Reverend William Tennent at Neshaminy, about twenty miles from Philadelphia. Tennent, a cousin to James Logan, had emigrated to America in 1718 with his wife and four children. A pastor at Neshaminy Presbyterian Church until his death in 1746, Tennent founded his Log College in 1726 or 1727. It lasted until 1742. Tennent's school, actually an academy and not a college, since it gave no degrees and had no charter, offered a tough curriculum consisting of theology, Greek, Latin, and the "arts and sciences." The Log College, which had a number of prominent graduates including John Blair and Samuel Finley, both of whom became presidents of Princeton University, served as the model for similar types of schools. Some of these schools—Samuel Blair's at Fagg's Manor and Robert Smith's at

Pequea, both in Pennsylvania; John Brown's in Augusta, Virginia; and David Caldwell's in North Carolina, for example—became well-known.

Tennent's Log College was the forerunner of other Presbyterian colleges and universities. The College of New Jersey in Princeton (now Princeton University) was founded in 1746 to train ministers in the way that Harvard and Yale Universities were doing for the Puritans of New England. Other colleges followed, including Hampden-Sidney in Virginia in 1776 and Washington and Jefferson in Pennsylvania in 1780. According to Leyburn, "Of the 207 prominent colleges established in the U.S. before the Civil War, fifty—by far the largest group—were begun by Presbyterians, mostly of Ulster adoption."[2]

Despite the growing number of schools, the Presbyterian Church failed to provide enough ministers to meet the spiritual needs of its congregations. During the eighteenth century, legions of Baptist and Methodist ministers poured into the backwoods, converting thousands of Scotch-Irish for whom the Presbyterian religion had been like a birthright. The frontier began to undergo a religious transformation in 1738 when the charismatic evangelist George Whitefield made the first of his seven visits to America and initiated the "Great Awakening." A brilliant orator, he spoke passionately to the hearts and not the minds of his listeners, setting colonial America ablaze with religious fervor. He traveled from Georgia to New England, drawing large crowds wherever he went and attracting many Presbyterian ministers and converts into his evangelical orbit.

The Great Awakening affected all denominations, but none as much as the Presbyterians. A division arose within the church: on the one side were the conservative Old Siders, who, as Leyburn says, "were contemptuous of Whitefield's pulpit pyro-technics, dubious of the validity of the sudden conversions he achieved, and sure that the church would degrade itself by diluting its message and making religion 'easy' for the common man,"[3] on the other side were the liberal New Siders, who believed that the church should try to speak to its members in their own language and adopt a missionary approach to meet the spiritual needs of the backcountry settlers. The split in the church lasted thirteen years.

Despite the controversy, the denomination grew, and like the Scotch-Irish people, Presbyterian Churches were eventually found in every colony. The Presbyteries directing church affairs extended throughout the colonies. Commenting on the legacy of the Presbyterian Church, Leyburn says that the "federal structure of the church of the Scotch-Irish seemed congenial to American conditions and exerted a unifying influence in our early history."[4]

Although arriving with little political experience, the Scotch-Irish made an impact on colonial politics, helping to end privilege and to establish more democratic provincial constitutions. Their contributions came primarily in Pennsylvania, Virginia, and North and South Carolina, where they were heavily concentrated. In none of the four colonies did their political participation follow the same pattern.

In Pennsylvania the Scotch-Irish were the last of the three major ethnic groups to settle. The Quakers, the largest group in the first half of the eighteenth century, held tight control over the colony's economic and political life. To protect their privileged position, the peace-loving Quakers had even encouraged the Scotch-Irish to move to the frontier, where they would be far away from the seat of power and could serve as a buffer against French or Indian attack. Politics mattered little to the Scotch-Irish during this period. They were too busy trying to establish themselves on the frontier.

The Scotch-Irish initiation into Pennsylvania politics came in 1754 with the outbreak of the French and Indian War. The fighting began over rival French and English claims for possession of the Ohio Valley. Many Indian tribes became allies of the French, who promised them the return of tribal lands.

Unlike the other colonies, Pennsylvania was totally unprepared for war. Safe in the eastern counties and far away from the fighting, the Quaker-controlled assembly showed little concern for the plight of the embattled frontiersmen and an unwillingness to provide troops and supplies. The Quakers were pacifists who believed that war was wrong and against the laws of God. The Scotch-Irish, however, could little afford to turn the other cheek. They were locked in a life-and-death struggle with the Indians. Frustrated and angry, Scotch-Irish leaders demanded action. A change in colonial policy did not come until 1756, when a concerned governor and council took matters into their own hands and officially declared war. In protest the Quakers boycotted the assembly.

The Scotch-Irish played a major role in defeating the Indians and in ending the French control of the Ohio Valley. Adapting Indian fighting methods, they took the offensive and made surprise attacks deep into Indian territory, catching the Indians off guard and helping to turn the tide of battle.

With Pontiac's defeat in 1763, peace returned to the frontier. Settlers began to pour into western Pennsylvania. Once again, however, trouble arose between the whites and the Indians. When the "Paxton Boys" killed twenty Conestoga Indians, the Quakers, who were back in political control of the colony, took steps to take all of the province's Indians under their protection. Outraged, the Scotch-Irish organized; they drew up a petition and sent a delegation of more than five hundred to Philadelphia to present it. Although unable to change Quaker policy, the Scotch-Irish continued to put steady political pressure on the Quaker-controlled provincial government up until the Revolution. They finally became the dominant element in Pennsylvania politics in 1776 when they allied themselves with the Germans and took control of the assembly.

Unlike Pennsylvania politics, Virginia politics during the colonial period proved to be less volatile and not divided on the basis of national origin. Although leadership for change came mainly from the Piedmont and Tidewater gentry, the Scotch-Irish of the Valley of Virginia became their staunch supporters in the fight against privilege and in the passage of a new liberal constitution.

No such alliance existed in North Carolina, where the legislature was controlled by the low-country planter aristocracy. The planters adopted a haughty attitude and discriminated against the upcountry settlements, where the Scotch-Irish predominated. One governor even referred to the backwoodsmen as "outcasts and fugitives of other colonies."[5] By the 1760s, the upcountry settlers began to complain openly about their treatment by the eastern establishment. When the authorities failed to address their grievances, the settlers decided to take the law into their own hands. The resulting "Regulator movement" was responsible for some killings, kidnappings, threats, and burnings of cabins. The situation did not return to normal until 1771 when troops sent by Governor William Tryon crushed the Regulators at the Battle of Alamance. Five leaders were hanged, and many Regulators fled across the mountains into eastern Tennessee. Most of the remaining Regulators received a pardon by Tryon's successor, Governor Martin, on condition that they take the oath of allegiance to the Crown.

In upcountry South Carolina, there was also a Regulator movement; however, its main grievance was not too much government but the appalling lack of governmental institutions provided by the low country authorities. The settlers' complaints were many—a lack of country organization, no local government and courts, no law enforcement, and the arduous journey that had to be made to Charles Town (present-day Charleston) to vote. In 1666 and 1667 upcountry settlers petitioned the Commons House of Assembly in Charles Towne for change. When their appeals fell on deaf ears, the settlers took the law into their own hands. They refused to pay taxes and even planned a march on Charles Towne to make their grievances known. The settlers finally began to get relief in 1772 when the authorities provided courts for the upcountry.

Until the outbreak of the Revolutionary War, the Scotch-Irish were concerned with politics in their own local communities and colonies. War with England, however, drew them into national affairs. Unlike some other groups—such as the Scots, who generally sided with the British, and the Dutch and Germans, who were divided in their opinion—the Scotch-Irish were strong supporters of the American Revolution. Even before the actual fighting broke out, the Scotch-Irish began to make a stand. In Westmoreland County, Pennsylvania, settlers became incensed at the news of Lexington and Concord, and they met at Hannastown, where they adopted five resolutions, which became known as the Westmoreland Declaration. In it, they declared their willingness to oppose British policy with their lives and fortunes.

In Clinton County, Pennsylvania, settlers adopted the Pine Creek Dedication, which expressed their support for the Declaration of Independence then under discussion in Congress. Communities in Virginia and North Carolina also approved resolutions. In Mecklenburg County, North Carolina, for example, militia companies sent representatives to Charlotte on May 20, 1775, to adopt the Mecklenburg Declaration of Independence, thus anticipating the Declaration of Independence by more than a year.

Numerous leaders and writers on both sides of the Atlantic commented on the Scotch-Irish involvement in the rebellion and on their fervent support of the patriot cause. In the British House of Commons, Horace Walpole said: "There is no use crying about the matter. America has run off with a Presbyterian parson and that is the end of it."[7] One British captain wrote in 1778: "Call this war what you may, only call it not an American rebellion. This is nothing less than a Scotch-Irish Presbyterian rebellion."[8] In Philadelphia, an Episcopalian loyalist declared that a "Presbyterian loyalist was a thing unheard of."[9]

Joseph Galloway was at first a delegate to the Continental Congress but later fled to England to join the British side. Called before a British committee investigating the composition of the American troops, he answered: "There were scarcely one-quarter of them natives of America. Half of them were Irish. The other quarter were English and Scotch."[10]

No fewer than five Scotch-Irish delegates—Thomas McKeon, Edward Rutledge, James Smith, George Taylor, and Mathew Thornton—signed the Declaration of Independence. The document is in the handwriting of Charles Thomson, an Ulster man from Maghera, County Londonderry, who was secretary of the congress that adopted the resolution. It was printed by John Dunlap of Strabane, County Tyrone, the founder of the country's first newspaper in 1791, the *Pennsylvania Packet*. And it was first read in public by Colonel John Nixson, whose father had come from Ireland.

Despite this impressive record, we would be wrong to conclude, as some glorifiers of the Scotch-Irish achievement have done, that the Scotch-Irish almost to a man supported the Revolutionary War or that their involvement was the sole reason for the patriot victory. The Scotch-Irish support came primarily in the colonies from Virginia northward and in one area of North Carolina. There was considerable loyalist sentiment in the Carolina Piedmont, while in Georgia the Scotch-Irish were little involved in the war. As historians have pointed out, despite the names associated with the Declaration of Independence, the Scotch-Irish contributed little to the ideology of the Revolution. A look at the names on the list of leaders guiding the war effort—most notably John Adams, Thomas Jefferson, and Benjamin Franklin—shows that they were nearly all of English or Scottish descent.

The Scotch-Irish contribution came on the battlefield, where their fighting ability and strong belief in the cause often made the difference. In Pennsylvania, thousands of Scotch-Irish heard the call to arms and joined the Continental Army—so many, in fact, that Light-Horse Harry Lee called the Pennsylvania line "the line of Ireland."[11] The Scotch-Irish formed the backbone of Washington's army, which remained steadfast through the trying winter at Valley Forge. Later, when the fighting extended to the frontier, the Scotch-Irish took up arms and helped turn the tide of battle. At the important Battle of King's Mountain on October 9, 1780, a patriot force composed mainly of Scotch-Irish attacked and defeated a British force twice its size, killing the British commander and 180 of his men and taking 1,000 prisoners.

During the early years of the new Republic, the Scotch-Irish continued to be politically active. The French Revolution was the subject of heated debate during the 1790s. It split the country between the Federalists, who supported England, and the Republicans, who sympathized with France. The Scotch-Irish, who had little love for the British, sided with the Republicans and helped organize pro-Republican clubs and militia units.

Many Scotch-Irish also agitated against Jay's Treaty, which they believed gave too many concessions to England. At a meeting in Philadelphia in July 1795, a Scotch-Irishman named Blair McClenachan, a leading citizen in town, led a group of angry citizens to the British minister's house, where the treaty was symbolically burned.

By the beginning of the nineteenth century, the Scotch-Irish were winning election to political offices at all levels of government. Many held distinguished and powerful positions. Henry Knox became a member of Washington's first cabinet. John Rutledge of South Carolina and Thomas McKeon of Pennsylvania were elected governors of their new state governments. When Andrew Jackson became president in 1828, the descendants of the Scotch-Irish who had emigrated almost a century before attained the highest office in the land.

During this formative period of the American Republic, however, the Scotch-Irish, like other immigrant groups, were ceasing to emphasize their ancestry. The memory of the life that their forefathers had known in Ireland had become dim with time. Those who continued to come from Ulster did not look for Scotch-Irish communities in which to settle. They went wherever the right opportunity presented itself. Many became part of the anonymous masses that crossed the mountains into the valleys of the Ohio and Mississippi Rivers, building the roads, clearing the wilderness, establishing the settlements, and pushing the frontier westward in a restless search for a better life. It is here, perhaps, that the Scotch-Irish can be "regarded as America's first true backwoodsmen, showing the way to the winning of the West, leading the vanguard who [crossed] the Alleghanies to open up for settlement that great valley in the heart of the continental U.S."[12]

From this point on, the Scotch-Irish began to make their contribution as Americans and not as Scotch-Irish—that is, not as people of a particular ethnic culture. They intermarried with other ethnic groups, mixing easily and eventually losing their identity as a separate people. By and large, the Scotch-Irish have become absorbed into the mainstream of society. There has been no real self-conscious effort to maintain their separate identity, as some other ethnic groups have done. Historically, though, the Scotch-Irish contributed much toward the making of America: establishing a major religion; giving impetus to elementary and higher education; helping to fight against political privilege; promoting democratic principles; supporting the War for Independence; and participating in the winning of the West. Today, people of Scotch-Irish ancestry can look with pride upon a record of achievement of service to the nation.

Appendix

Scotch-Irish Sites of Historical Interest in the North of Ireland

Andrew Jackson Center

Located in County Antrim, this site contains the ancestral home of Andrew Jackson, seventh president of the United States (1829–37), whose family emigrated to the United States in 1765 from Carrickfergus, northern Ireland. The Jackson family members, originally settlers or planters of the Oliver Cromwell period, had moved to the Carrickfergus district from County Kildare, Ireland. Where the president was born remains the subject of controversy, with Jackson himself once saying, "I was born somewhere between Carrickfergus and the United States."

Arthur Ancestral Home

Located in County Antrim, this restored eighteenth-century farmhouse with an open, flax-straw, thatched roof is the ancestral home of Chester Alan Arthur, twenty-first president of the United States (1881–85). Arthur's father left his farmhouse at Cullybackey in 1815 and set sail for America. Chester Arthur was born in 1830 and became the last first-generation American to become a U.S. president.

Ballygally Castle

Located on the Antrim Coast Road, this castle looks across the sea to Scotland, where the roots of its builder, James Shaw, and the style of construction are found. Shaw came from Greenock in Scotland and built the castle in about 1625. The castle is one of Northern Ireland's few remaining seventeenth-century buildings still in use.

Carrickfergus Castle

Located at County Antrim at the town of Carrickfergus, this castle was the first real castle built in Ireland. Its massive structure was believed to be started in 1180 by John DeCourcy or by Hugh de Lacy and was finished in the mid-thirteenth century. In 1315 the castle was captured after a year's siege by the forces of the Scottish Robert and Earl Bruce, but it was retaken in 1318 by the English, who held on to it for the next three hundred years.

William of Orange landed here on June 14, 1690, and a large stone marks the place where he stepped ashore. In 1778, American John Paul Jones fought a naval engagement off the coast of Carrickfergus. Carrickfergus remained garrisoned until 1928. The castle houses an exhibit of the castle's history, as well as a shop, a café, and a visitor's center.

Dalway's Bawn

On the coast road to Ballycarry, this structure, which was owned by John Dalway, is an usually well preserved example of an early-seventeenth-century planter's fortified enclosure. Dalway surrounded himself with this stone bawn in about 1609 to secure his royal grant of land in the area.

Dunluce Castle

Located two to three miles from Portrush in County Antrim, these dramatic ruins are located on a rocky headland. Most of the castle dates from the sixteenth and seventeenth centuries; the oldest part, dating from the late thirteenth century or the first years of the fourteenth century, still survives and stands on a huge rock, joined to the mainland only by the narrow top of an arched wall. Dunluce is believed to have been built in about 1300 by Richard de Burgh, earl of Ulster. In 1642, General Robert Munro paid what was intended to be a family visit to Dunluce, but he seized the castle and made its owner, Randal MacDonnell, a prisoner. The castle was subsequently abandoned and fell into decay, although it is a popular tourist attraction today.

Giant's Causeway

This rock formation, extending from the Antrim Coast to the island of Skye in Scotland, is one of the world's most interesting geological formations. It was formed by the cooling of the lava that burst through the earth's crust in the Cenozoic period. The lava's cooling resulted in the splitting of the basaltic rock into innumerable prismatic columns. Various sections of the formation have been given names—The Organ, The Chimney Pots, and Lord Antrim's Parlor, among others.

Grant Ancestral Home

John Simpson, the great-grandfather of Ulysses S. Grant, eighteenth president (1869–1877), was born in this house in 1738. It is located in Auchnacloy, County Tyrone.

Gray's Printing Press

This press is located on Main Street in Strabane, County Tyrone, in an elegant shop front. John Dunlap, a Scotch-Irishman, began his apprenticeship at Gray's before leaving for Philadelphia in 1756 at age ten. He later founded the first newspaper in America and printed the first copies of the Declaration of Independence from Thomas Jefferson's manuscript. James Wilson, grandfather of Woodrow Wilson, twenty-eighth U.S. president (1913–21), also served an apprenticeship here. Visitors to Gray's can see some interesting examples of the early printing press.

Linenhall Library

Founded in 1788 as the Belfast Reading Room, this library is the oldest cultural institution in Belfast and is renowned for its preservation of books and other materials of Irish interest.

Public Records Office of Northern Ireland (Proni)

Located at 66 Balmoral Avenue, PRONI is the most important institution in Northern Ireland for visitors wanting to learn more about their Scotch-Irish roots. Established in 1923, the office has millions of documents extending from about 1600 to the present and includes records of government departments, courts of law, local authorities, and nongovernmental public bodies, as well as records deposited by churches, businesses, and private individuals. For further information, contact PRONI at 66 Balmoral Avenue, Belfast BT9 6NY, Northern Ireland.

Springhill

Located in County Londonderry near Moneymore on the Moneymore-Coagh road, this manor house was built by "Good" Will Cunningham when he married Miss Ann Upton in 1680. It includes gardens, family belongings, a costume museum, and woodland walks. As a guide published by the National Trust of Northern Ireland described Springhill, "It is a house of enormous simple charm, and the warm atmosphere of the old wood in the interiors is not dissipated by the fact that Springhill boasts one of the best authenticated ghosts in an Ulster House—seemingly a mother who lost seven children through smallpox still moves there."[1]

Ulster-American Folk Park

Located in County Tyrone at Castletown, this park is an outdoor museum designed to tell the story of emigration to North America in the eighteenth and nineteenth centuries. Its layout depicts the various aspects of the emigrant's life on both sides of the Atlantic Ocean and features a unique display of outdoor exhibits with many original buildings, such as the ancestral homes of Thomas Mellon, John Joseph Hughes, and Robert Campbell.

The Mellon home stands on its original site. Other highlights include a typical weaver's cottage, in which a nineteenth-century weaver would have lived and worked; a meetinghouse, which is a replica of the Presbyterian Church at Mountjoy in which Thomas Mellon worshipped; and a log cabin, the type of house that early immigrants like Thomas Mellon occupied when they first arrived in America.

Ulster Folk and Transport Museum

Situated on the main Belfast-to-Bangor Road, just ten minutes outside Belfast, this museum contains many exhibits with illustrative themes, such as pottery, craft tools, folk customs, and agricultural techniques, and town and country houses that have been moved from their original settings in various parts of Ulster and rebuilt on the museum grounds. Some of the buildings—the Weaver's House, the Spade Mill, and the Flax Scrutching Mill— give examples of equipment used, as well as insights into how people worked in past centuries. Here, visitors can buy books and homemade objects relating to various aspects of Ulster's past.

Walls of Derry

These famous walls have withstood many sieges, including the most famous siege: 105 days in 1689. The old walls are in good condition, and a visitor can follow a path around them while inspecting the cannons used during the various sieges. On the Royal Bastion stands the Walker Monument, a ninety-foot column surmounted by a statue of the clergyman George Walker.

The Wilson House

On the slopes of the Sperrin Mountains at Dergalt in County Tyrone is located the ancestral home of James Wilson, the grandfather of President Woodrow Wilson, Nobel Prize winner and twenty-eighth president of the United States (1913–21). The house, a simple building that contains original furniture, is typical of the type of home an Ulster emigrant occupied before leaving for America in the eighteenth and nineteenth centuries.

Born on February 20, 1787, James Wilson emigrated to America as a young man of twenty in 1807. He had been trained as a printer in Ulster but became a prominent newspaperman in America, settling in Philadelphia and founding the newspaper *The Pennsylvania Advocate*, in 1832.

Notes

Prologue

1. Christopher Buckley, "The Old Money That Built It," *Esquire*, June 6, 1978, p. 36.
2. "Another 'Mellon House' in Pittsburg," *Conestoga: Newsletter of the Ulster-American Folk Park*, Spring 1997, p. 1.
3. "Thomas Mellon," *National Cyclopedia of American Biography* (New York: J. T. White, 1891–1984), vol. 28, p. 335.
4. Thomas Mellon, *Thomas Mellon and His Times* (Pittsburgh: University of Pittsburgh Press, 1994), p. 5.
5. Ibid., p. 7.
6. Ibid., p. 22.
7. Ibid., p. 37.
8. Ibid.
9. "Thomas Mellon."
10. "Another 'Mellon House' in Pittsburg," p. 1.
11. Kathleen Neill, "Irish-Scotch Ancestry," *British Heritage*, (no month) 1984, p. 54. The other U.S. presidents are James Buchanan, Grover Cleveland, Ulysses S. Grant, Benjamin Harrison, James Knox Polk, and Woodrow Wilson.
12. "Back to the Old Sod," *Time*, June 28, 1968, p. 48.

Chapter 1

1. James E. Handley, *The Irish in Scotland, 1798–1845* (Cork, Ireland: Cork University Press, 1943), p. 3.

2. John Bannerman, *Studies in the History of Dalriada* (Edinburgh: Scottish Academic Press, 1974), p. 9.

3. Ian Adamson, *The Identity of Ulster* (Belfast: W & G Baird, 1982), p. 5.

4. Although the vast woodlands have now vanished, at the time of the coming of the Scottish settlers to Ireland in the early seventeenth century, 15 percent of the total area of Ireland was forested. Ruth Dudley Edwards, *An Atlas of Irish History* (London: Methuen and Co., 1973), p. 3.

5. Forty of Niall's descendants succeeded him as high king. They took the title of Ui Neil, which they retained to the fifth century. J. Anderson Black, *Your Irish Ancestors* (Secaucus, N.J.: Castle Books, 1980), p. 25.

6. Graham Ritchie and Anna Ritchie, *Scotland: Archaeology and Early History* (New York: Thomas and Hudson, 1981), p. 87.

7. Bannerman, *Studies in the History of Dalriada*, p. 79.

8. John Prabble, *Lion of the North: A Personal View of Scotland's History* (New York: Cowans, McAnn, and Geoghagen, 1971), p. 18.

9. Allen Kent and Harold Lancour, *Encyclopedia of Library and Information Science* (New York: M. Decker, 1968), p. 69.

10. John Ranelagh, *Ireland: An Illustrated History* (New York: Oxford University Press, 1981), pp. 60–61.

11. Ibid., p. 41.

12. G. A. Hayes-McCoy, *Scot Mercenary Forces in Ireland, 1565–1603* (Dublin: Burns Oats, 1937), p. 41.

13. Ibid.

14. Ranelagh, *Ireland,* p. 71.

15. Bannerman, *Studies in the History of Dalriada*, p. 79.

16. Constantine Fitzgibbon, *The Irish in Ireland* (New York: W. W. Norton, 1983), p. 113.

17. Robert Kee, *Ireland: A History* (Boston: Little, Brown and Company, 1980), p. 30.

Chapter 2

1. M. Perceval-Maxwell, *The Scottish Migration in Ulster in the Reign of James I* (New York: Humanities Press, 1973), p. 17.

2. Ibid., p. 78.

3. Charles Hanna, *The Scotch-Irish,* 2 vols. (New York: Putnam, 1902), 1:495.

4. Ibid., 1:486.

5. Eventually all of O'Neill's remaining lands were sold to Hamilton, Hugh Montgomery, and other proprietors. James G. Leyburn, *The Scotch-Irish: A Social History* (Chapel Hill: University of North Carolina Press, 1962), pp. 87–88.

6. T. W. Moody, *The Londonderry Plantation* (Belfast: William Maldan and Son, 1939), p. 28.

7. Public Records Office of Northern Ireland, *Educational Facsimile Series: The Plantations of Ulster* (Belfast: Public Records Office of Northern Ireland, 1975), p. 5.

8. Ibid., p. 2.

9. Perceval-Maxwell, *Scottish Migration in Ulster*, p. 118.

10. Leyburn, *The Scotch-Irish*, p. 95.

11. Perceval-Maxwell, *Scottish Migration in Ulster*, p. 135.

12. In all, there were six plantation surveys conducted during the reign of James I.

13. Perceval-Maxwell, *Scottish Migration in Ulster*, p. 126.

14. Ibid., p. 41.

15. James G. Leyburn, "The Melting Pot: The Ethnic Group That Blended the Scotch-Irish," *American Heritage Illustrated* 22 (1970): 28–31, 97–101.

16. Perceval-Maxwell, *Scottish Migration in Ulster*, p. 278.

17. A. T. A. Stewart, *The Narrow Ground* (London: Faber and Faber, 1977), p. 81.

18. Ibid., pp. 81–82.

19. James Henry Ford, *The Scotch-Irish in America* (Princeton: Princeton University Press, 1915) p. 123.

20. Perceval-Maxwell, *Scottish Migration in Ulster*, p. 152.

21. Ford, *The Scotch-Irish in America*, p. 123.

22. Moody, *The Londonderry Plantation*, p. 40.

23. Perceval-Maxwell, *The Scottish Migration in Ulster*, pp. 211–12.

24. Ibid.

25. Ibid., p. 217.

26. Moody, *The Londonderry Plantation*, p. 23.

27. Leyburn, *The Scotch-Irish*, p. 102.

28. Public Records Office of Northern Ireland: Educational Facimile Series, p. 10.

29. Ibid., p. 10.

30. Perveval-Maxwell, *Scottish Migration in Ulster*, p. 307.

Chapter 3

1. James G. Leyburn, *The Scotch-Irish: A Social History* (Chapel Hill: University of North Carolina Press, 1962), p. 54.

2. Ibid., p. 52.

3. Ibid., p. 50.

4. M. Perceval-Maxwell, *The Scottish Migration in Ulster in the Reign of James I* (New York: Humanities Press, 1973), p. 152.

5. Charles Hanna, *The Scotch-Irish*, 2 vols. (New York: Putnam, 1902), 1:416.

6. Leyburn, *The Scotch-Irish*, p. 117.

7. Hanna, *The Scotch-Irish*, 1:440.

8. Leyburn, *The Scotch-Irish*, p. 120.

9. James B. Woodburn, *The Ulster Scot: His History and Religion* (London: Allenson, 1914), p. 96.

10. Ibid., p. 92.

11. J. Anderson Black, *Your Irish Ancestors* (Secaucus, N.J.: Castle Books, 1980), p. 93.

12. David Stephenson, *Scottish Covenanters and Irish Confederates* (Belfast: Ulster Historical Foundation, 1981), p. 295.

13. T. W. Moody, "The Irish and Scotch-Irish in Eighteenth-Century America," *Studies* 35 (1946): 85.

14. Hanna, *The Scotch-Irish*, 1:445.

15. Black, *Your Irish Ancestors*, p. 96.

16. Richard Broad et al., *The Troubles* (London: Thames, MacDonald Futura, 1981), p. 13.

17. Ibid., p. 13.

18. Hanna, *The Scotch-Irish*, 1:452.

19. J. M. Barkley, *A Short History of the Presbyterian Church in Ireland* (Belfast: Presbyterian Church of Ireland, 1959), p. 14.

20. Tony Gray, *No Surrender* (London: MacDonald and James, 1975), p. 29.

21. Leyburn, *The Scotch-Irish*, p. 126.

22. Barkley, *A Short History*, p. 15.

23. Margaret Dickson Falley, *Irish and Scotch-Irish Ancestral Research* (Baltimore: Genealogical Publishing Company, 1981), p. 389.

Chapter 4

1. Tony Gray, *No Surrender* (London: MacDonald and James, 1975), p. 40.

2. Thomas Witherow, *Derry and Enniskillen in the Year 1689* (Belfast: William Mullan, 1873), pp. 21–22.

3. Maury Klein, "The Scotch-Irish," *American History Illustrated* 14 (1979):34.

4. Witherow, *Derry and Enniskillen*, p. 149.

5. Gray, *No Surrender*, p. 71.

6. Ibid., p. 104.

7. Ibid., p. 105.

8. Ibid., pp. 80–88.

9. Ibid., p. 93.

10. Ibid., pp. 97-98.

11. Ibid., p. 157.

12. Cedil David Milligan, *History of the Siege of Derry* (Belfast: H. L. Carter Publications, 1951), p. 73.

13. Ibid.

14. Gray, *No Surrender*, pp. 176, 180–181.

Chapter 5

1. A. C. Anderson, *The Story of the Presbyterian Church in Ireland* (Belfast: Bell, Logan, and Coswell, 1950), p. 23.

2. J. Harrison, *The Scot in Ulster* (Edinburgh: Blackwood and Sons, 1888).

3. James G. Leyburn, *The Scotch-Irish: A Social History* (Chapel Hill: University of North Carolina Press, 1962).

4. R. J. Dickson, *Ulster Emigration to Colonial America, 1718–1775* (Belfast: Ulster Historical Foundation, 1976), p. 7

5. Ibid., p. 8.

6. Ibid., p. 9.

7. Ibid., p. 14.

8. Leyburn, *The Scotch-Irish*, p. 163.

9. Ibid.

10. Tyler Blethen and Curtis Wood Jr., *From Ulster to Carolina: The Migration of the Scotch-Irish to Southwestern North Carolina* (Cullowhee, N.C.: Mountain Heritage Center, Western Carolina University, 1983), p. 16.

11. Dickson, *Ulster Emigration*, p. 24.

12. T. W. Moody, *The Ulster Question* (Dublin: Mercer Press, 1980).

13. Not all Scotch-Irish emigrated to America. Some returned to Scotland; others went to England, France, Germany, Spain, and even the West Indies.
14. James G. Leyburn, "Presbyterian Immigrants and the American Revolution," *Journal of Presbyterian History* 54 (1979): 27.
15. W. F. Marshall, *Ulster Sails West* (Belfast: Quota Press, 1943), p. 20.
16. Ibid.
17. Dickson, *Ulster Emigration*, p. 35.
18. Dickson, *Ulster Emigration*, p. 47.
19. Ibid., p. 55.
20. Leyburn, *The Scotch-Irish*, p. 178.
21. Wayland F. Dunaway, *The Scotch-Irish of Colonial Pennsylvania* (Baltimore: Genealogical Publishing Company, 1979), p. 73.
22. Ibid., p. 77.
23. Dickson, *Ulster Emigration*, p. 79.
24. Leyburn, *The Scotch-Irish*, p. 188.
25. R.J. Dickson, *Ulster Emigration to Colonial America 1718–1775*, p. 21.
26. Ibid., p. 27.
27. James G. Leyburn, *The Scotch-Irish: A Social History*, p. 221.

Chapter 6

1. James G. Leyburn, *The Scotch-Irish: A Social History* (Chapel Hill: University of North Carolina Press, 1962), p. 152.
2. Richard Hofstadter, "The Americans," *American History Illustrated* 6 (1971): 43.
3. R. J. Dickson, *Ulster Emigration to Colonial America, 1718–1775* (Belfast: Ulster Historic Foundation, 1976), p. 23.
4. Leyburn, *The Scotch-Irish*, p. 190.
5. Wayland F. Dunaway, *The Scotch-Irish of Colonial Pennsylvania* (Baltimore: Genealogical Publishing Company, 1979), p. 36.
6. T. W. Moody, "The Irish and Scotch-Irish in Eighteenth-Century America." *Studies* 35 (1946): 21.
7. Leyburn, *The Scotch-Irish*, p. 199.
8. Dunaway, *The Scotch-Irish of Colonial Pennsylvania*, p. 71.
9. Maury Klein, "The Scotch-Irish," *American History Illustrated* 10 (1979): 36.

10. Dunaway, *The Scotch-Irish of Colonial Pennsylvania*, p. 59.
11. Ibid.
12. Leyburn, *The Scotch-Irish*, p. 205.
13. Dunaway, *The Scotch-Irish of Colonial Pennsylvania*, p. 113.
14. Klein, "The Scotch-Irish," p. 37.
15. Ibid.
16. Leyburn, *The Scotch-Irish*, p. 227.
17. Ibid., pp. 216–17.
18. Ibid., p. 233.
19. Ibid., p. 235.

Chapter 7

1. E. Estyn Evans, "The Scotch-Irish: Their Cultural Adaptation," in E. R. R. Greene, ed., *Essays in Scotch-Irish History* (New York: Rutledge and Kegan Paul, 1969), p. 78.

2. Wayland F. Dunaway, *The Scotch-Irish of Colonial Pennsylvania* (Baltimore: Genealogical Publishing Company, 1979), p. 184.

3. Evans, "The Scotch-Irish," p. 81.

4. Dunaway, *The Scotch-Irish of Colonial Pennsylvania*, p. 171.

5. Ibid., p. 188.

6. Maury Klein, "The Scotch-Irish," *American History Illustrated* 14 (1979): 15–17.

7. James G. Leyburn, *The Scotch-Irish: A Social History* (Chapel Hill: University of North Carolina Press, 1962), p. 264.

8. Dunaway, *The Scotch-Irish of Colonial Pennsylvania*, pp. 197–98.

9. Leyburn, *The Scotch-Irish*, p. 292.

10. Dunaway, *The Scotch-Irish of Colonial Pennsylvania*, pp. 209–10.

Chapter 8

1. James G. Leyburn, "Presbyterian Immigrants and the American Revolution," *Journal of Presbyterian History* 54 (1979): 14.

2. James G. Leyburn, *The Scotch-Irish: A Social History* (Chapel Hill: University of North Carolina Press, 1962), p. 324.

3. Ibid., p. 279.

4. James G. Leyburn, "The Melting Pot: The Ethnic Group That Blended the Scotch-Irish," *American Heritage Illustrated* 22 (1970): 101.

5. James G. Leyburn, "The Scotch-Irish," *American Heritage Illustrated* 22 (1970):301.

6. Leyburn, *The Scotch-Irish,* p. 301.

7. Wayland F. Dunaway, *The Scotch-Irish of Colonial Pennsylvania* (Baltimore: Genealogical Publishing Company, 1979), p. 156.

8. Maury Klein, "The Scotch-Irish." *American History Illustrated* 14 (1979): 15.

9. Ibid.

10. W. F. Marshall, *Ulster Sails West* (Belfast: Quota Press, 1943), p. 37.

11. Dunaway, *The Scotch-Irish of Colonial Pennsylvania,* p. 156.

12. Leyburn, *The Scotch-Irish,* p. 256.

Appendix

1. National Trust of Northern Ireland, *Ulster Heritage: A Tour of the Properties of the National Trust of Northern Ireland* (Belfast: National Trust of Northern Ireland, 1978), p. 10.

Bibliography

Adair, P. *A True Narrative of the Rise and Progress of the Presbyterian Church in Ireland (1623–1670)*. Belfast: Aitchison Press, 1866.

Adamson, Ian. *Cruithin: The Ancient Kindred*. Newtownards, Northern Ireland: Nosmada Books, 1974.

Alexander, Samuel D. *History of the Presbyterian Church in Ireland*. New York: Robert Carter and Brothers, 1860.

Anderson, A. C. *The Story of the Presbyterian Church in Ireland*. Belfast: Bell, Logan, and Coswell, 1950.

_____. "Another 'Mellon House' in Pittsburg." *Conestoga: The Newsletter of the Ulster-American Folk Park*, Spring 1997.

Bannerman, John. *Studies in the History of Dalriada*. Edinburgh: Scottish Academic Press, 1974.

Barkley, J. M. *A Short History of the Presbyterian Church in Ireland*. Belfast: Presbyterian Church of Ireland, 1959.

Beckett, J. C. and R. E. Glasscock, eds. *Origin and Growth of an Industrial City*. Belfast: W. J. Mackey and Company, 1967.

Bigger, F. J. "From Uladh to Gallway and from Gallway to Uladh." *Red Hand Magazine* 6 (November 1920).

Black, J. Anderson. *Your Irish Ancestors*. Secaucus, N.J.: Castle Books, 1980.

Blethen, Tyler, and Curtis Wood, Jr. *From Ulster to Carolina: The Migration of the Scotch-Irish to Southwestern North Carolina*. Cullowhee, N.C.: Mountain Heritage Center, Western Carolina University, 1983.

Bolton, Charles K. *Scotch-Irish Pioneers in Ulster and America*. Baltimore: Genealogical Publishing Company, 1981.

Bibliography

Broad, Richard, et al. *The Troubles*. London: Thames, MacDonald Futura, 1981.

Brooks, John. *Ulster's Heritage*. Dublin: Eason's and Sons, 1978.

Burke's Peerage. *Burke's Presidential Families of the United States of America*. London: Burke's Peerage, 1975.

Chadvick, H. M. *Early Scotland: The Picts, the Scots, and the Welsh of Southern Scotland*. London: Cambridge University Press, 1949.

Chart, D. A., ed. *A Preliminary Survey of the Ancient Monuments of Northern Ireland*. Belfast: Her Majesty's Stationery Office, 1940.

Chauvire. *A Short History of Ireland*. New York: New American Library, 1966.

Colles, Ramsey. *History of Ulster from Earliest Times to the Present Day*. Belfast: Gresham Publishing Company, 1969.

Cromie, Howard. *Ulster Settlers in America*. Belfast: T. H. Jordan, 1977.

Curtayne, Alice. *The Irish Story: A Survey of Irish History and Culture*. New York: P. J. Kennedy and Sons, 1960.

DeBreffney, Brian. *Castles of Ireland*. London: Thames and Hudson, 1977.

Dickson, R. J. *Ulster Emigration to Colonial America, 1718–1775*. Belfast: Ulster Historical Foundation, 1976.

Dunaway, Wayland F. *The Scotch-Irish of Colonial Pennsylvania*. Baltimore: Genealogical Publishing Company, 1979.

Edwards, Ruth Dudley. *An Atlas of Irish History*. London: Methuen and Company, 1973.

_____. *Facts about Ireland*. Dublin: Department of Foreign Affairs, 1981.

Falley, Margaret Dickson. *Irish and Scottish-Irish Ancestral Research: A Guide to the Genealogical Records, Methods, and Sources to Ireland*. Baltimore: Genealogical Publishing Company, 1981.

Ford, James Henry. *The Scotch-Irish in America*. Princeton: Princeton University Press, 1915.

Glasgow, Maude. *The Scotch-Irish in Northern Ireland and the American Colonies*. New York: G. P. Putnam's Sons, 1936.

Gray, Tony. *No Surrender*. London: MacDonald and James, 1975.

Green, E. R. R., ed. *Essays in Scotch-Irish History*. New York: Rutledge and Kegan Paul, 1969.

Hamilton, C. J. "Scotland, Ireland, and the English Civil Wars." *Albion* (Appalachian State University) 7 (1975).

Handley, James E. *The Irish in Scotland, 1798–1845*. Cork: Cork University Press, 1943.

Hanna, Charles. *The Scotch-Irish*. 2 vols. New York: Putnam, 1902.

Hansen, M. L. *The Atlantic Migration, 1607–1800: A History of the Continuing Settlement of the United States*. Cambridge: Harvard University Press, 1940.

Harrison, J. *The Scot in Ulster*. Edinburgh: Blackwood and Sons, 1888.

Hayes-McCoy, G. A. *Scot Mercenary Forces in Ireland, 1565–1603*. Dublin: Burns Oats, 1937.

Hayward, Richard. *Belfast through the Ages*. Dundalk: Dundalgan Press, 1952.

_____. *In Praise of Ulster*. Belfast: Arthur Barker, 1938.

_____. *Ulster and the City of Belfast*. London: Arthur Barker, 1950.

Henry, P. L. *Ulster Dialects*. Belfast: Ulster Folk Museum, 1969.

Hill, George. *An Historical Account of the MacDonalds of Antrim*. Belfast: Archer and Sons, 1973.

Hofstadter, Richard. "The Americans." *American History Illustrated* 6 (1971).

_____. *Illustrated Ireland Guide*. Dublin: Bord Failte Eireann, 1967.

_____. *Ireland Guide*. Dublin: Bord Failte Eireann, 1976.

Johnson, James E. *The Scots and the Scotch-Irish in America*. New York: Lerner Publications, 1966.

Jope, F. M. "Fortification to Architecture in the North of Ireland." *Ulster Journal of Archaeology* 23, 3d ser. (1960).

Kee, Robert. *Ireland: A History*. Boston: Little, Brown and Company, 1980.

Kerr, W. S. *Walker of Derry*. Londonderry: Sentinel, 1938.

Killanin, Lord, and Michael V. Dunigan. *The Shell Guide to Ireland*. London: Ebury Press, 1967.

Bibliography

Klein, Maury. "The Scotch-Irish." *American History Illustrated* 9, 10, and 14 (1979).

Lawlor, Henry C. *Dunluce and the Route.* Belfast: Linehall Press, 1919.

Leash, Harold G. *Irish Castles and Castellated Houses.* Dundalk: Dundalgan Press, 1964.

Lehmann, William Christian. *Scottish and Scotch-Irish Contributions to Early American Life and Culture.* Port Washington, N.Y.: National University Publications, 1977.

Leyburn, James G. "The Melting Pot: The Ethnic Group That Blended the Scotch-Irish." *American Heritage Illustrated* 22 (1970).

_____. "Presbyterian Immigrants and the American Revolution." *Journal of Presbyterian History* 54 (1979).

_____. "The Scotch-Irish." *American Heritage Illustrated* 22 (1970).

_____. *The Scotch-Irish: A Social History.* Chapel Hill: University of North Carolina Press, 1962.

McCaffery, Lawrence J. *Ireland from Colony to Nation.* Englewood Cliffs, N.J.: Prentice Hall, 1979.

MacDonald, Colin M. *The History of Argyle up to the Beginning of the Sixteenth Century.* Glasgow: W. R. Holmes, 1950.

Montgomery, Eric. *The Ulster-American Folk Park: How It All Began.* Omagh: Scotch-Irish Trust of Ulster, n.d.

_____. *The National Cyclopedia of American Biography.* New York: J. T. White, 1891–1984.

National Trust of Northern Ireland. *Ulster Heritage: A Tour of the Properties of the National Trust of Northern Ireland.* Belfast: National Trust of Northern Ireland, 1978.

Perceval-Maxwell, M. *The Scottish Migration in Ulster in the Reign of James I.* New York: Humanities Press, 1973.

Prabble, John. *Lion of the North: A Personal View of Scotland's History.* New York: Cowans, McAnn, and Geoghagen, 1971.

Public Records Office of Northern Ireland. *Educational Facsimile Series: The Plantations of Ulster.* Belfast: Public Records Office of Northern Ireland, 1975.

Bibliography

Ranelagh, John. *Ireland: An Illustrated History.* New York: Oxford University Press, 1981.

Ritchie, Graham, and Anna Ritchie. *Scotland: Archaeology and Early History.* New York: Thomas and Hudson, 1981.

Woodburn, James B. *The Ulster Scot: His History and Religion.* London: Allenson, 1914.

Index

Index